AF496756

AN ENGLISH ANTHOLOGY
PART II. NOTES AND INDICES

SIR HENRY NEWBOLT'S
AN ENGLISH ANTHOLOGY

SHOWING THE MAIN STREAM OF ENGLISH LITERATURE FROM THE FOURTEENTH TO THE NINETEENTH CENTURY.

Second Impression.

"It is indeed no excessive claim that 'shining pieces have gone by hundreds into this mosaic.' It is an inexhaustible delight to turn these leaves at random. . . . In these thousand pages there is store for the leisure hours of a lifetime."—*The Morning Post.*

In this book Sir Henry Newbolt gives us a selection of English Prose and Verse from the fourteenth to the nineteenth century. The book has been compiled for the use of teachers and students of English: its object is to show the progress of the English language and literature as the gradual gathering of a great concourse of characters and influences. The total effect of this concourse at any moment is made clear by the arrangement. The authors included are placed, not by order of birth, but by the dates at which their first or most decisive work appeared. By this arrangement the reader will gain an idea of the effective content of the literary mind at any given date, and will be able to make his own observation of the influence of great writers or great events upon the generations which followed them.

PART II. NOTES AND INDICES
By Sir Henry Newbolt

This book is issued as a companion to the above volume. It contains critical and appreciative comments on the authors and their works, and should be found especially valuable for students.

AN ENGLISH ANTHOLOGY OF PROSE AND POETRY

(14TH CENTURY–19TH CENTURY)

PART II. NOTES AND INDICES

COMPILED BY

HENRY NEWBOLT

1922

LONDON & TORONTO

J. M. DENT & SONS LTD.

NEW YORK: E. P. DUTTON & CO.

INTRODUCTION

THE purpose of this *English Anthology* is " to show the progress of the English language and literature as the gradual gathering of many tributaries into one stream, or of many characters and influences into one great national concourse." It places every writer therefore, not by the date of his birth— the moment of birth is not the moment of his effective entry into the world of thought—but by the date at which he may be judged to have arrived in the concourse as a conspicuous or influential member of it. The reader is invited to open the book wherever he will and imagine himself to be the contemporary of the author there exemplified: he will be able to get some idea from the preceding pages of what might then have formed the literary content of his mind, and in the succeeding pages he can look forward to that which was still in the future. This is a convenient way of applying the Historic Method: but in suggesting it I am anxious not to give a mistaken view of the relation of History and Literature.

A work of art—a piece of literature—is not the subject of History in any but a very limited way: it is not the product of an Organism or a Process, in the biological sense, but the unique, timeless expression of a spirit in a world of spirits. This timelessness of Art cannot be too clearly stated or too constantly remembered. The worlds of Chaucer, Shakespeare, Keats, Byron, Browning—and even of much lesser and less fertile poets — are all unique, separate, self-existent worlds, each created for the first time and by the act of a single person. But they are created by a transmuting power, out of experiences afforded by the world of every day. The components of these experiences have a history, which may be known and stated, in terms of Time or succession, and even of Causation.

The Time is obvious, but less important than the Causation. Man being what he is, a spirit and member of a society of spirits, can only express himself as such; that is, in forms addressed to or intelligible by others of his kind. Literary art, therefore, is the intercourse of choicer spirits, in which they receive and give experiences: and it is often intercourse which extends beyond the bounds of an age or a national society. The experience of one (or of many) becomes part of the experience of another (or others), and through them of yet others. The gradual onward flow of these transmitted experiences is like a broadening stream: it flows through the whole landscape, and no one, however original, can be wholly unaffected by it.

But originality does not depend on freedom from influences. (It could not, for everyone has an environment, and one resulting from the past.) These influences, this tradition of methods and insight, this store of experiences, is a strength, not a weakness, for those who can use it with a degree of mastery. There will always be, as Mr. Abercrombie says, " the amateur artist who worries himself with anxiety to create beauty "—that is, the man who, being fond of figs, wishes to be a fig tree as well as a consumer—but there will also be the genuine artist whose impulse and vision are his own, though he receives from others the suggestion of a subject, a vocabulary, a technique, or even the first guidance towards a new point of view. His feeling, too, will inevitably be coloured by the social and political life of his country and by the public or semi-public opinion of his generation: and it is on this account that private letters, diaries, and other non-literary documents have been included in our collection.

We may speak then of the history of literature if we please: but let us at the same time remember what Literature really is: let us look at the work of the great initiators and note that the greater they are the more difficult or the less relevant it is to define them in such terms. When we make our survey of literature we are not inspecting a pedigree herd or a school of verbal dexterity: what we see is the spectacle of the timeless, immaterial human spirit expressing itself under the limitations of Time and bodily existence. We too are under those limitations, and we find a reasonable pleasure in comparing and placing the work of individual artists: but we shall gain a greater experience of sympathy, insight and wonder in proportion as we realise that the artist, though always a person, is not in his essential reality a temporal, a national or an individual being.

One more word of warning is necessary. There are several periods in which the tributaries of our great stream flow in in very rapid succession. When a number of authors are " arriving " close together dates should be exact: and this is sometimes very difficult to ensure. I have gone over the whole list with the aid of *The Dictionary of National Biography*, the huge *Record of English Literature* of Dr. Garnett and Mr. Edmund Gosse, Professor Saintsbury's *History of English Literature* and Professor Elton's *Survey of English Literature*. All these are admirable books, and their differences add to the reader's pleasure—except when they disagree as to dates. They frequently vary by one year, not infrequently by three; and not possessing first editions of the whole company of English writers myself, I have been forced at times to find a verdict on the evidence instead of recording a scientific fact. In three cases (out of 230) I have had to confess mistakes, and these shall some day be remedied. But the arrangement, in spite of any small inaccuracies, will be found to justify itself. It will be noted, on looking down the column of " arrival dates," that there are some remarkable years or short periods—e.g. the period 1590–94, 1610–13, 1710–13, 1817–19, or 1832–33—when a kind of spate came down the stream. To a contemporary, or one living a few years later, or to us now, such periods must have a wonderful appearance— they were great times to be alive in. But write down these same authors or tributaries in the order of their birth-dates and the spate disappears: while on the other hand, when births coincide (*e.g.* in 1829), neither in fact nor in contemporary effect is there anything to admire at all. Lastly the method over-rides the " grouping " of writers by the specific form of their writings: and that alone is worth doing: for there is no doubt that this device has hitherto saved the historian's time and trouble rather than the reader's.

NOTE

The year which *precedes* each author's name is that assigned as the date of his " arrival "—that is, of the decisive appearance of his fame or influence in the world of letters. The facts by which the date is fixed are given in the note which follows; but strict uniformity cannot be secured. The sky may be clear for one star; another may rise in mist and only be visible some time afterwards, but its influence may be as great as that of North upon Shakespeare or Phineas Fletcher upon Milton.

AN ENGLISH ANTHOLOGY OF PROSE AND POETRY

13th Century. Poetry before Chaucer

The long and illustrious line of the English poets may truly be said to have been founded by Chaucer, as a family is said to be founded by that ancestor who first established it in a fixed place and influence. But like every such founder, Chaucer too had origins, and these four pieces are inserted here to give some indication of their nature. His narrative poetry owed little to any English progenitor, but it is clear that he was not the first, by a good century, to write English lyrics, nor is it to him that we owe the adaptation to our own speech of the lyric models of the troubadours and trouvères of France.

The Cuckoo Song, which is generally ascribed to the middle of the thirteenth century but may be somewhat earlier, is the first English song of which we possess the original music (British Museum—for two, three, or four voices and chorus), and as verse " the first perfectly delightful thing in English poetry " (Saintsbury).

Alison is the best piece in a MS. collection also in the British Museum (Harleian MSS. 2253). It is specially interesting for its evident descent from the old English alliterative mode as well as from the Anglo-Norman rhymed lyric.

The winter song This World's Joy, ascribed, like *Alison*, to the end of the thirteenth century, is even more modern in feeling and in cadence. Any reader who has succeeded in mastering the language and disregarding the obsolete spelling will appreciate the perfection of the workmanship. The final line anticipates the last-line effect of the Spenserian stanza.

A   I

ROBERT MANNING was a Gilbertine canon, born at Brunne (Bourn) in Lincolnshire. His date is not certainly known, but he was writing in 1320 and lived into the reign of Edward III. His work is remarkable for the introduction not only of French words, but of French terminations and constructions.

1362. William Langland

LANGLAND is placed here not as a progenitor of Chaucer but as an elder contemporary—an elder brother, it might be said, of equal rank, but of less fruitful genius. It was not from him that the English poets were to derive: his great poem (1362) was " the consummation of that strictly national style of poetry . . . which, having been carried by him to the utmost height of which it was capable, is about to yield to a more perfect form of art, as Ennius and Lucilius of old gave place to Virgil and Horace " (R. Garnett).

1369. Geoffrey Chaucer (1340?–1400) (I.)

THE two extracts here given represent CHAUCER's work in what are known as his French and Italian periods. Examples of his English period follow under the date 1388.

THE BOOK OF THE DUCHESSE is probably the earliest of Chaucer's extant poems: it is dated by the death of Blanche, Duchess of Lancaster, who died in September 1369, and upon whom the elegy is written; under the influence of the French poets.

TROILUS AND CRISEYDE appears (from the style and the use of the rhyme royal) to have been written between 1379 and 1382: certainly after one or both of his journeys to Italy (1373 and 1378). It owes much to Boccaccio's *Filostrato*, and was in turn the source of Henryson's *Testament of Cressid*, and of Shakespeare's *Troilus and Cressida*, and Dryden's adaptation of the same.

1372-7. John Wyclif (1320?-1384)

It is not certain that the APOLOGY FOR LOLLARD DOCTRINES
is by Wyclif.   It is, however, included in a contemporary MS.
volume which contains many of the treatises commonly attributed to him; and there are in it no passages or quotations
inconsistent with a belief in his authorship.   The extract is
taken from James H. Todd's edition (Camden Society, 1842).
Wyclif's influence was well established by 1372, and in that
year he took the degree of Doctor in Divinity.

1378-84. The Wyclif Bible (1378-84)

THE WYCLIF BIBLE, the first English translation, was made
(1378-84) from the Vulgate by Wyclif and two other Oxford
scholars, Nicholas of Hereford and John Purvey.   It is often
defective as a translation, but its influence upon the English
nation and language cannot be overestimated.   It formed, directly
and indirectly, one of the sources of all the great versions which
followed it, and the sound of its magnificent cadences was carried
by them all into the Authorised Version.   A comparison of the
passages here given with the parallels from Coverdale and the
Authorised Version (pp. 115-20 and 286-8) will show that the
music of our greatest prose is essentially the music of the Wyclif
Bible, and that in places where it had been destroyed in the
labour of more accurate translation from the Hebrew, it was often
restored again in the final version.   One example may be given:
Wyclif wrote in Isaiah xxxv., " they schulen have joy and gladness, and sorrow and wailing schulen flee away."   In Coverdale
this becomes, " pleasure and gladness shall be among them.
And as for all sorrow and heaviness, it shall vanish away."   But
in the Authorised Version it reappears in its original beauty: " they
shall obtain joy and gladness, and sorrow and sighing shall flee
away."   The Psalms, on the other hand, lost little and gained
much in Coverdale's hands, and it is mainly to him that we
owe the version used every day in the Book of Common Prayer.

1388. Geoffrey Chaucer (II.)

It was necessary for the purpose of this compilation to separate Chaucer's work into two parts, showing the rise of two different streams of influence. " *Troilus and Criseyde* is indeed epochmaking in a sense, but in a purely literary sense. With it the Italian element enters English poetry, to its signal improvement and refinement. But with *The Canterbury Tales* the English people enter, and poetry becomes truly national " (R. Garnett). 1387 is the year in which the pilgrims are supposed to start for Canterbury, and part at any rate of the poem is shown to have been composed not later than 1388, by the mention of Middleburg in Holland as the seat of the wool-staple. But parts are perhaps earlier. In *The Legend of Good Women* (1385) Chaucer says that he has already written " al the love of Palamon and Arcyte," and there are lines in *The Knight's Tale* which show beyond question that this story was not originally intended for *The Canterbury Tales,* but adapted later for the purpose. Again, the story of Griselda is told by the Clerk of Oxenford, who says he got it at Padua, from " Frauncys Petrak the laureat poete ": and in fact it was in 1373, when Chaucer was first in Italy, that Petrarch made a translation of it into Latin from Boccaccio's original. Whether Chaucer then saw the Italian MS. or not, his debt to it is plain.

The division is also justified by the reputed influence of Wyclif on Chaucer; a tradition very consistent with the pictures of churchmen and church officials drawn and coloured in *The Canterbury Tales*. Such an influence could only have taken effect after Chaucer's earlier poems were written, but must have come before 1388; and this is here shown by the order.

1390. John Gower (1325?–1408)

Gower was in years probably rather older than Chaucer, but as an influence he must be placed later, both as Chaucer's confessed disciple and because his only achievement in English poetry, the *Confessio Amantis,* was not completed until 1390. It contains, among many other stories, the tale of Florent, told also by Chaucer as *The Wife of Bath's Tale,* and the tale of Emarë or Constance, which is *The Man of Law's Tale* in *The Canterbury Tales,* and is there prefaced by a remarkable speech on Chaucer's own work, with a side-glance at the *Confessio Amantis.* It is clear from this that Chaucer had read Gower's work before it was completed, and it is a possible inference that he borrowed the two stories from it; but it may equally well be that the two friends had read the old romances together, and that their choice of material coincided in these two cases, though Chaucer's taste rejected (as the Man of Law says) others which were not too strong for the " moral Gower."

In any case Gower's reputation and influence were very great: though far inferior to Chaucer in genius, he was his coadjutor in the formation of English as a literary language. His enormous poem—it has more lines than Homer—was the first English poem ever translated into other languages; and in England its influence is seen in the work of many poets, including Shakespeare (see the Prologue to *Pericles,* Act I.).

1399.   Richard the Redeless (Author uncertain—1399)

The attribution of RICHARD THE REDELESS (1399) to Langland is doubtful—Professor Saintsbury says " one of the least doubtful of such things," but the vocabulary is different and the peculiarly vigorous humour still more so. The pungent realism of this picture of the House of Commons, if it comes from the author of *Piers Plowman,* would give us a new idea of his poetical range. On the other hand it is not easy to imagine that Langland had a contemporary who used the same style with such effect, and yet left nothing but this fragment of 870 lines. The extract here given is from the edition of Thomas Wright (Camden Society, 1838).

c. 1425.   John Lydgate (1370?–1451)

LYDGATE (like his " less accomplished double," Hoccleve, for whom we have no room here) was a professed disciple, imitator, and continuator of Chaucer: and though he is a much inferior

story-teller he has something of his English humour and delight
in the characters of men, as well as in the pleasures of the
country. He is a less accomplished verse writer than Gower,
but to a modern reader far better worth the trouble. He is
known to have produced important work between 1412 and 1430.

c. 1425. Sir John Mandeville (14th Century)

"SIR JOHN MANDEVILLE" was almost certainly the pseudonym
of an Englishman named John de Burgoyne or Bourgignon, who
died at Liège in 1372; but he was hardly an English author,
for his book of Travels (1356) was written originally in French
and only translated into English (from a Latin version) after
his death. The date is not known, but it is certainly not later
than 1430, and may be as early as 1400. Its popularity in the
mediæval world was unparalleled—the three hundred MS. copies
which survive include versions in twelve European languages—
and its importance as a model can hardly be overestimated: "it
is the first book of *belles lettres* in English prose" (Saintsbury).

Chester Plays

THE CHESTER PLAYS were not printed until 1591, but they are
ascribed to the fourteenth century, or possibly the thirteenth.
Conjecture based on the inflectional forms of words is made
doubtful by the fact that they are irregularly used, and the
text may have been tampered with by copyists: the spelling
is certainly late.

1424-37. James I. of Scotland (1394-1437)

The immediate following of Chaucer was stronger in Scotland
than in England. *The Kingis Quhair* is not only Chaucerian,
and supremely elegant, but it lifts the spring-song of love from

the instrumental music of words to the ecstasy of a new vision. Though the type of the poem, and its language—a mixture of northern and southern dialects—are of a marked fourteenth-century brand, such a passage as that here quoted belongs to the poetry which is timeless. King James died in 1437.

1452. The Paston Letters

THE PASTON LETTERS are not, in the strict sense, literature, but they exhibit with great vividness the life of the English in the fifteenth century, and thereby form an invaluable link between the age of Chaucer and Langland and the age of the Tudors. They should be remembered side by side with Malory's *Morte Darthur* in any estimate of English character. As historical material for literature they have been used by several novelists: last by R. L. Stevenson, who borrowed from the proceedings concerning Robert Ledham (1452), here extracted, the greenwood part of *The Black Arrow* and some of the names of his characters, with many other hints. It is difficult now (as perhaps in 1452) to make out whether Ledham himself, or Roger Chirche, was actually John Amend-all.

In the Eton boy's letter the figure of the squire's younger brother in his search for a wife appears for the first time in English.

c. 1462. Robert Henryson (15th Century)

HENRYSON is the second great Scottish poet of the Chaucerian School. Dr. Garnett calls him " a genius, who with one aspect looks back to Chaucer, with the other forwards to Burns and Allan Ramsay." He was probably born about 1421, but there is nothing to fix his date, except the fact that he was admitted to Glasgow University in 1462 as "Venerabilis vir Magister Robert Henryson ": the title-page of his book (long after his death) calls him " Schoolmaster in Dunfermline." The poem here given is the first pastoral poem or eclogue in English.

THE PILGRIMS' VOYAGE is the earliest sea song in English; but it is not the first appearance of the sea tradition. See the description of the Shipman in *The Canterbury Tales* (Prologue) and the nautical metaphors in the last three lines of the extract from *Richard the Redeless* (1399, p. 38). There are also (though not here) two poems by Lawrence Minot, dated 1352, on the victories of Sluys and " Les Espagnols sur Mer ": republished by Professor Firth in his *Naval Songs and Ballads* (Navy Record Society, 1907).

CAXTON printed and published his translation of *The Recuyell of the Histories of Troye* in 1474, but the memory of his excellent prose has been kept alive by his edition of Malory, which he printed, with his own Proem, in 1484. Malory's own reputation dates from the same event and year, though the *Morte Darthur* was actually completed in 1469.

This piece is the best proof that SKELTON could write gracefully: in the main he was a jovial burlesque poet, who, like Butler (1663, p. 391), " wrote doggerel with genius." Caxton in 1490 speaks of him as Poet Laureate in the University of Oxford.

DUNBAR is the third great poet of Scotland, and fully the equal of King James and Robert Henryson. His praise of London has a kind of Biblical splendour and fervour almost rivalling the praise of the New Jerusalem by the unknown E. B. P. at the end of the sixteenth century.

The LAMENT FOR THE MAKERS is a fine example of the Latin *refrain*, and of great literary interest from its references to Chaucer, Gower and the rest. His poem to Margaret of England was presented in 1503, and a volume of his poems was printed in 1508.

Anonymous Poetry (15th and 16th Centuries)

These anonymous poems are all undated, and are here grouped together for convenience, at the turn of the century. GOSSIP MINE is a picture of English manners, and the first poem on the great national theme of Drink, which was only touched incidentally by the author of *Piers Plowman* (*Gula*, in Passus V.), and by Chaucer when introducing the drunken Miller in *The Canterbury Tales*.

QUIA AMORE LANGUEO is the first and greatest religious lyric in English.

THE NUT-BROWN MAID was first published in 1502. " The ring and swing of the metre, of which no previous example seems to exist . . . the tenderness and sweetness . . . the dramatic management of the story, and the modest cogency of the moral," make it, as Professor Saintsbury says, " a pearl of poetry for ever." It seems to have been beyond imitation by any later poet, but its repute has been great and fruitful.

The two pieces which follow continue the tradition of the English Greenwood, which is not merely " literary " but human and national. Robin Hood is the hero of a great number of ballads: his last effective reappearance was in the early nineteenth century, in Scott's *Ivanhoe* and Peacock's *Maid Marian*.

1523? Stephen Hawes

STEPHEN HAWES, whose dates are unknown, continued the Chaucerian tradition in the early sixteenth century, and seems to be feeling his way towards a Spenserian kind of allegory. In a single passage of his one remembered poem he struck a bell whose tone has never ceased to vibrate.

1523. Lord Berners (1467–1533)

JOHN BOURCHIER, LORD BERNERS, as a translator of French romance is the counterpart of Malory, a gifted writer of prose, but historically rather than poetically chivalrous. His style is highly personal and highly accomplished; its secrets remain unexhausted to this day. William Morris drew upon Berners' *Froissart* (1523) in his prose and verse: in *The Hollow Land* and *The Dream of John Ball*; in *Love is Enough* and in the Prologue to *The Earthly Paradise*.

1531. Sir Thomas Elyot (1490?–1546)

With *The Governour* (1531) begins the long list of English treatises on Education. Next comes Cheke, a pedant (1514–57), and then Ascham, a distinguished prig (1514–68), who feared art and literature: there is no room here for either.

1516–1535 (1551). Sir Thomas More (1478–1535)

MORE'S *Utopia* was written in Latin (1516), published abroad, and not translated until sixteen years after his death; its influence, therefore, must have been gradual, and effective not upon the style of his successors, but upon their thought. It was profound and lasting. *Cf.* Bacon's *New Atlantis*, 1627; Harrington's *Oceana*, 1656; Bellamy's *Looking Backward*, 1889; William Morris's *News from Nowhere*, 1890; W. D. Howells' *A Traveller from Altruria*, 1894; H. G. Wells's *A Modern Utopia*, 1905.

1535. The Coverdale Bible

MILES COVERDALE (1488–1568), sometime Bishop of Exeter, was the translator of this version of the Bible (1535), the first ever published in England. (Henry VIII.'s Commission had in 1530 reported in favour of a new translation being made, but against its being issued to the public.) The "Matthew Bible" of 1537 incorporated Coverdale's, which was also again used in the preparation of Cranmer's "Great Bible," 1539. Coverdale was thus, though not a zealot, fortunate and persevering enough to succeed, where Tyndale perished, in the struggle against the Papal party for the publication of the Bible in England. 1535 is therefore a crucial point in the history of the English language.

"We cannot undo the past. English Literature will ever *have been* Protestant " (Cardinal Newman).

1540? Sir Thomas Wyatt (1503–42)

1540? Henry Howard, Earl of Surrey (1517?–47)

The poems of WYATT and SURREY can only be dated conjecturally. Wyatt was the elder by about fifteen years and has been described as standing to Surrey in the relation of master to pupil; but the work of both shows the same origin and development, as though it were the result of a joint trade with Italian poetry, carried on by two partners who had both gone to school to Chaucer. Their most remarkable imports into England were the sonnet, and (in Surrey's case) blank verse. In Surrey's translation of Virgil here given, lines like

> Unto the son of Venus, the goddes,

and

> Long to furrow large space of stormy seas

are as Italian and as Chaucerian as some of the ten-syllable lines in Wyatt's sonnets:

> With his hardiness takes displeasure.

But Surrey's work is an advance: there is a wider stretch between Wyatt's sonnets and Shakespeare's than between Surrey's *Virgil* and *Paradise Lost*. Rhythms such as

> Holding backward the steps where we had come
> In the dark night, looking all round about

are exactly paralleled by Milton, who was not working in the dark.

1563. John Foxe (1516–87)

The English Literature, as Cardinal Newman said, is historically a Protestant Literature; and Foxe's *Acts and Monuments* (1563) (known significantly as Foxe's *Book of Martyrs*), had an immense effect on the mind and emotion of sixteenth and seventeenth-century England.

1570–80? William Cecil, Lord Burleigh (1520–1598)

BURLEIGH'S name was a synonym for grave wisdom. He appears here as a Polonius, sententious and commonplace, but on his own plane irrefutable. The *Precepts* are, like *The Paston Letters*, documents rather than literature: but they read like an anticipation of Bacon's *Essays*:

"Be not served with kinsmen, or friends, or men intreated to stay; for they expect much and do little; nor with such as are amorous, for their heads are intoxicated." *Cf.* pp. 236–7.

The *Precepts* must have been written during the early youth of "son Robert," whose dates are not certainly known, but who is stated to have entered at Cambridge in 1581.

1572. John Knox (1505–72)

KNOX is another great Puritan influence; but a political and controversial writer rather than a man of letters. His one great book, *The History of the Reformation in Scotland*, appeared after his death in 1572.

1576. Raphael Holinshed (1525–78)

HOLINSHED is a chronicler with more distinction in his style than most of his class. But his importance to literature lies mainly in the copious material which he supplied to Shakespeare for his historical plays; and even his phrases often reappear in glory. His *Chronicle* was published in 1576.

1579. Sir Thomas North (1535?–1601?)

NORTH's translation of Plutarch (1579) was a strong reinforcement of the classical influence in England, and was quarried for moral sentiments and political and patriotic examples by successive generations. It supplied also the material for Shakespeare's classical plays and no insignificant part of their magnanimity. Compare the passage here given with Shakespeare's transmutation of it, on pp. 237–43.

1579. John Lyly (1554?–1606?)

LYLY's essay on education is contained in his *Anatomy of Wit* (1579), but forms a separate division under the title of *Euphues and his Ephebus*. It is based on Plutarch's treatise.

Lyly's prose was a deliberate attempt to create a highly ornate style in English, according with the high-flown spirit of the time. It was followed up by Lodge and Philip Sidney (*Arcadia*); but faded before the more dignified and personal art of Drummond of Hawthornden and Sir Thomas Browne. The Euphuist fashion was parodied by Shakespeare in *Love's Labour's Lost* and by Sir Walter Scott in *The Monastery*, Chapter X., a sketch imitated from Ben Jonson's *Every Man out of his Humour*, Act IV. Scene vi., and after all Lyly is read to-day with a new admiration. He was also an accomplished lyrical poet, and the author of romantic plays which lead on to the Forest of Arden and the wood of the *Midsummer Night's Dream*.

1588. Sir Francis Drake (1545-96)

If we had no more than these two letters we should still know much of the fight with the Armada, of Drake, of English patriotism, and of the English sea service. But beyond this they have the style of the age and the man. The paragraph of the "orange trees" belongs to the literature of history. The intensive understatement in "some grief" (*cf.* Shakespeare's "Some danger!") is characteristically English, and has been widely revived during the war, 1914-18.

1589. Robert Greene (1560-92)

Swinburne has remarked that in *Richard II.* the spirits of Greene and Marlowe "are visibly contending for the mastery of Shakespeare's poetic and dramatic adolescence." The lines here given show where Shakespeare learnt the trick of interspersing his blank verse with rhymed couplets; and in *Love's Labour's Lost* the use of other metres in dialogue is clearly traceable to the influence of the same writer; but the resemblance extends further, to the imagination and tone of country scenes and humour. Greene's *Friar Bacon* was produced in 1589.

The remarkable outburst called A LAST WARNING is famous for its clear reference to Shakespeare and his relation to his better educated rivals in playwriting. "There is an upstart crow, beautified with our feathers, that with his *tiger's heart wrapt in a player's hide* supposes he is as well able to bombast out a blank verse as the best of you; and being an absolute *Johannes factotum,* is in his own conceit the only *Shakescene* in a country." The "tiger's heart" line is parodied from one in Shakespeare's 3 *Henry VI.* (I. iv. 137).

1590. George Peele (1558ſ-97ſ)

PEELE was another of the "University Wits." His blank verse is at least as good as Greene's, but had less effect; his lyrics are better. The *Farewell to Arms* has for three centuries helped to keep fresh the musical note of chivalry. It was written in 1590.

1590. Edmund Spenser (1552?–99)

PAGE

The palace of SPENSER's mind was adorned by collections from many poets, Latin, Italian, and English. *The Shepherd's Calendar* is the work of one who remembers Virgil, Chaucer, and *Piers Plowman*. The February part of it, *The Oak and the Brere*, is in a metre which Spenser may have made for himself, or taken (as Professor Saintsbury thinks) from an early paraphrase of *Genesis and Exodus*; and it may again have been borrowed or reinvented by Coleridge for his *Christabel*. If we have here a series of influences or bequests, it is a remarkable one, stretching from the thirteenth to the nineteenth century.

The " Spenserian stanza " used in *The Faery Queen* may also have been Spenser's own discovery, achieved by adding a long ninth line to one of the Italian eight-line forms. The peculiar effect of this might well have been suggested by the final line of the stanza in the anonymous thirteenth-century poem *This World's Joy*. (See above, *English Anthology*, p. 3.) A similar use is found in the *Epithalamion*. *The Faery Queen* marks Spenser's full tide as 1590, the year in which he returned with it from Ireland.

1590. Thomas Lodge (1556–1625?)

LODGE's affinity is proclaimed by the second title of his *Rosalynde, Euphues' Golden Legacie*: he was, like Lyly, a satirist and playwright, and an experimenter in romantic prose. *Rosalynde* (1590) is a novel, which gave Shakespeare not only the material, but nearly the whole material for his *As You Like It*; and a detailed comparison of the two is indispensable for any student of Shakespeare's dramatic method. The *Madrigal* here given is the most admirable of the lyrics interspersed in the story.

1591. Sir Philip Sidney (1554–86)

SIR PHILIP SIDNEY was a brilliant Euphuist who died in 1586 at the height of an almost unequalled reputation; but the influence of his literary work must be dated from its posthumous publication. *Astrophel and Stella* was printed in 1591; the *Defence of Poesie* (*Apology for Poetrie*) in 1595. The former is the first example of a series of English sonnets written in accordance with the rule given in the famous line, " Fool, said my Muse to me, look in thy heart and write." The *Dirge* (included in the same work) gave Tennyson the first note of his " Ring out, wild bells," and one of the sonnets is echoed in the same poet's line, " And if you kissed her feet a thousand years."

The DEFENCE OF POESIE is in a somewhat ornate and wandering style, but it often moves the heart " more than with a trumpet," and is always of great interest for its theory, or theories, of poetry. Wordsworth must have approved the remarks on " rhyming and versing " (*English Anthology*, p. 179), and Pope those on verse and " the knitting up of the memory " (p. 180).

1591. Thomas Campion (1567?–1619)

CAMPION was a learned theorist in verse writing, and published some " Observations on the Art of English Poesy." The practical result was the mastery of rhythms quite peculiar to himself and specially suited for musical use. The various collections in the Elizabethan song books, of which Campion's are the finest numbers, form a region of poetry hardly entered these two hundred years past: in which the words call up and are themselves transformed by the sound of instruments no longer in our hands. Carew and Herrick had the touch of this art; but it seems to have died with our musical supremacy.

One of Campion's most beautiful lyrics (" Hark all you ladies that do sleep ") was published without his name in an appendix to Sidney's *Astrophel and Stella*. His *Books of Airs* followed in 1601–17.

1592. Sir Walter Raleigh (1552?-1618)

RALEIGH'S prose marks the sobering effect of " real " life and misfortune upon the typical Elizabethan. Even in his *Revenge*, written as early as 1592, he shows a singular restraint and gravity; in his *History of the World* he proclaims sea-power as the first principle of Empire; and in his final poem he is as religious and as resigned as any Puritan.

1592. Samuel Daniel (1562-1619)

DANIEL'S sonnet-sequence to *Delia* (1592) was one of the first to follow Sidney's *Astrophel and Stella*. (The numbers are of unequal value, and these four are decidedly better than most of them.) The fashion spread rapidly; and it is difficult to believe that Shakespeare was not following it when he wrote his sonnets: that he gave them no personal name does not prove that they are without connection or order.

1592. Christopher Marlowe (1564-93)

" MARLOWE'S mighty line " was the instrument of a dramatic genius, but his technique was not even so advanced as Surrey's and came nowhere near Shakespeare's—he did not live long enough to learn that the paragraph and not the single line is the true rhythmical unit of blank verse. But his spirit, in Swinburne's judgment, conquered Greene's in the struggle for the mastery of Shakespeare. The passage from his *Edward II.* (?1592) may be usefully compared with the abdication scene in *Richard II.*; but it does not prove, as some have maintained, that the earlier play is the greater. Intensity is Marlowe's strength, till it becomes his weakness; and posterity has forgotten his titanic plays for those of a more human and less mortal genius. His *Hero and Leander* survives because in a story of love and death intensity can hardly seem extravagant or unnatural.

B

1593. Richard Hooker (1554–1600)

HOOKER'S is a classical and monumental style, but it is the perfect expression of the man who wrote it: sincere and humane, learned and lively, broad and massive, patriotic and well balanced; adorned with fine phrases but only with such as arise naturally from the matter and the appropriate mood. A comparison with the work of any or all of the Euphuists will show the importance of Hooker to the modern prose of history, science and politics. The first edition (four books) of *The Laws of Ecclesiastical Polity* was licensed in 1593; the fifth book appeared in 1597, and the remainder after Hooker's death.

1594. William Shakespeare (I.) (1564–1616)

SHAKESPEARE'S " apprentice " years were ended by 1594, and *Richard II.* is the first play of his " great comedy " period: see notes on Greene and Marlowe, *supra*, for the influences under which it was written. The speech of Gaunt as the dying English patriot, has had an unending reverberation.

ROMEO AND JULIET is assigned to 1596: the dialogue in the flatter passages (*e.g. English Anthology*, p. 205), and the abundant rhyming couplets, are still reminiscent of Greene. Plot and characters are partly borrowed from a poem by one Broke, called *Romeus and Juliett*. The Sonnets were not published till 1609, but they must belong to this period.

1594. Michael Drayton (1563–1631)

DRAYTON'S sonnet-sequence *Idea* appeared in 1594, and was reprinted with additional numbers in 1599, 1602, 1605, and 1619. The sonnet here given is one of those added in 1619

and *is* infinitely his best.   Its authorship has been disputed, but
without proof. *Agincourt*, again, is much the best of his historical
and patriotic poems, and evidently set the time for Tennyson's
Charge of the Light Brigade. It was itself apparently founded on
an older ballad (" Agincourt, Agincourt, know ye not Agincourt ")
of considerable merit, which may be found in *War-Songs*, by
Christopher Stone and General Sir Ian Hamilton.

1598. Richard Hakluyt (1552?-1616)

HAKLUYT'S huge collection appeared in 1598, after an incuba-
tion which no doubt covered the whole sea life of Drake and
his contemporary adventurers. It is the muniment chest of the
English sea service: Hakluyt himself contributes little enough
in his own hand, but writes an excellent style in a spirit so
characteristically English as to appear almost an anachronism.

1598. Francis Meres (1565-1647)

MERES, though no great writer, rendered an immense service
to literature when he recorded his estimate of the English poets
and especially of those of his own time. The less remarkable
the man himself, the better is his evidence of contemporary
opinion.

The COMPARATIVE DISCOURSE (1598) names Shakespeare eight
times, and the inferences which may be drawn are many and
obvious. The date of twelve plays is thus fixed before 1598:
and some if not all of the Sonnets fall within the same line.
The testimony to Shakespeare's acknowledged supremacy is the
more convincing because it is not pressed. His name appears
four times in lists where he is placed almost indiscriminately
among a number of others: once he is given alone as the reincarnation of " the wittie sweete soule of Ovid "; once as
among our best poets for comedy; and once as the most excellent
in both kinds (comedy and tragedy) for the stage. Incidentally
is added the memorable sentence that " the Muses would speak
with Shakespeare's fine filed phrase, if they would speak English."

Anonymous Songs and Ballads of the 16th or early 17th Century

The first of these pieces is of unknown date. It used to be generally ascribed to Sir Walter Raleigh, but without good reason: it is of too distinctive beauty to be by any of the well-known poets.

Quotations from the *Song of Mary* or versions of it have been included in many hymnals; but for some curious reason the best stanzas—notably the one beginning " Thy gardens and thy gallant walks " — have almost always been among those omitted. The three remaining pieces come from the Elizabethan song-books, already remarked upon under Campion (1591).

1597. Francis Bacon (1561–1626)

BACON'S *Essays* began to appear in 1597, but were added to in later editions. The *Advancement of Learning* was published in 1605. These two passages are selected in order to suggest a comparison between Baconian and Shakespearean Poetry and Love. Bacon wrote a little verse, which has survived: neither it nor his " Account of Poetry " could have come from the author of the Shakespearean poems and plays. The impossibility of gathering figs from thistles (however fine and nutritious) is still clearer when the Essay on Love is read immediately before the scene which follows from *Antony and Cleopatra*—the extreme of prosaic common sense, materialistic and moralistic, contrasted with the extreme of unsparing passion and poetic vision.

1598. William Shakespeare (II.)

It was necessary to divide SHAKESPEARE's work into two parts under two separate dates, not because the nature of his influence changed materially after it had been once established, but because it would not otherwise have been possible to put Meres and Bacon in their right places with regard to him. This second period runs from 1598 to 1611 and includes all the great comedies and tragedies.

In 1614, two years before his death, he was addressed as follows by Thomas Freeman in his *Rubbe and a Great Cast*:

> Shakespeare, that nimble Mercury thy braine
> Lulls many hundred Argus-eyes asleepe,
> So fit for all thou fashionest thy vaine,
> At th' horse-foote fountaine thou hast drunk full deepe,
> Vertue's or vice's theme to thee all one is. . . .
> Besides, in plaies thy wit windes like Meander;
> When needy new composers borrow more
> Than Terence doth from Plautus or Menander.
> But to praise thee aright I want thy store.

1599. Richard Barnefield (1574–1627)

BARNEFIELD's one good poem is so good and so famous that a place must be found for it. Its effect may be judged from the fact that it was formerly supposed to be by Shakespeare. It first appeared anonymously in *The Passionate Pilgrim* (1599).

1599. Ben Jonson (1573–1637)

BEN JONSON's name was made by 1599, for *Every Man in his Humour* was acted by Shakespeare at the " Globe " before the end of 1598. He was a greater man to his contemporaries than he can ever be to later generations. His plays are learned and original, but they lead nowhere; they are for an age, not for all time; and to all but antiquarians they are dull. His lyrics are elegant and often felicitous, but never inspired. They have had, however, a considerable popularity and some influence. To one of them—the " Elegy " here given—Tennyson seems to have owed the metre of *In Memoriam*. The little " Epitaph " is so charming that Jonson was for generations credited also with William Browne's lines on the Countess of Pembroke—" Sidney's sister, Pembroke's mother " (*English Anthology*, p. 295). The lines " To the Memory of my Beloved Master William Shakspeare," prefixed to the First Folio (1623), are uneven but of the highest interest and reputation.

c. 1600. Ballads (Authorship unknown)

" THE BALLADS " are of unknown date; the place here assigned is that to which their final literary form seems to entitle them. Of their origin there are four different theories: one proclaims them to be " communal "—*i.e.* put together from the impromptu verses contributed by players in a round game. Another makes them traditional and degenerate versions of poems by the mediæval romancers: a third attributes them to poets of the fifteenth century, who did not care to place them among their acknowledged work. The fourth opinion—that of Professor Gummere—is that they were made by single authors and brought to their present form by those who handed them down in succession.

This theory alone would account for both their poetic mastery and their epic view of life in a primitive or half-civilised community. In them are mingled in an extraordinary degree courage and tenderness, pity and stark realism—the sense of a world full of tragedy, significance, and heroic beauty. Their singularity lies in their artistic form and diction—the latter long inherited and partially outworn, the former still vital and ready to the hand that can use it. Their influence has been very great: they have kept alive a tradition akin to the chivalrous but distinct from it, and they have from time to time carried their influence into literature—they haunted the memory of Shakespeare, stirred the heart of Sidney, and inspired both the poetry and the prose of Walter Scott.

1610–12. John Donne (1573–1631)

DONNE is a supreme example of the poet who hands on incomparably more than he received. He summed up many influences of the Elizabethan age, but transmitted to posterity an expression of them more modern by three hundred years than the work of any of his contemporaries. Naturally, therefore, he has been regarded by many as a revolutionary or a decadent; and by some the ruin of English verse has been laid to his charge. On the other hand his admirers count him among the few still living forces of the past. There is no middle position: admirable or regrettable, Donne is a portent, the sudden revelation of the human mind as no simple substance but the union and unrest of a multitude of atoms: a scene not merely of conflicting motives but of co-existing and contending personalities. He is, at the same time and in the same extreme degree, mystical and melancholy, sensual and tender, witty and uncouth, subtle and tremendously direct, brutally satirical and profoundly religious. Experience of such a range and depth belonged no doubt to Shakespeare too—his elder by only nine years—but in Shakespeare's plays it was subdued to the harmony of an art beyond Donne: it lies concealed in that immense charity as in the normal life of human society.

There are many modern poets who cannot be read without a recollection of Donne: Browning for example, and Meredith; and of the later generation Rupert Brooke, who felt himself to be not merely Donne's disciple but a reincarnation of his spirit.

Donne began to publish prose in 1610, and verse in 1611 (*An Anatomy of the World*), but the bulk of his poems were only printed after his death.

1610. Thomas Dekker (1575–1641)

The full muster of the English dramatists could only be represented by a series of lengthy extracts, which would alone suffice for a separate anthology. Dekker is among those whose plays must here be passed over; but his songs are good enough to keep his name in remembrance, even beside those of Shakespeare and Fletcher. Little is known of his life, though he collaborated with Ford, Massinger, and others; but his work. was all done by 1610.

1610. Giles Fletcher (158?–1623)

GILES FLETCHER (the Younger), son of Giles the author of the sonnet-sequence *Licia*, was a follower of Spenser, but with a special intensity and magnificence of his own. His metaphysical passages match Donne's: compare his conception of a timeless spiritual existence in these pages, with the last ten lines from the *Anatomy of the World* on the page before (*English Anthology*, pp. 284–5 with p. 283). *Christ's Victory* was published in 1610.

1611. Authorised Version of the Bible

After "Coverdale's Bible" (1535) came the "Matthew Bible" (1537) by Tyndale and Coverdale, the "Great Bible" or "Cranmer's Bible" (1539), the "Genevan Bible," a Puritan revision (1558), and the "Bishops' Bible" (1568). Finally a new translation to secure uniformity was proposed in 1604 by Dr. John Reynolds, President of Corpus Christi College, Oxford, and the king gave his immediate support. The work was carried out by forty-six scholars and divines, among whom were prominent Dr. Reynolds himself, Dr. John Spenser, his successor as President of Corpus, and Dr. Miles Smith, Bishop of Gloucester, sometime member of the same college (as was also Daniel Fairclough, another of the Oxford committee). Of these, Dr. Spenser had edited and

prefaced Hooker's *Ecclesiastical Polity*, and Dr. Smith wrote
the Dedication and Preface to the "Authorised Version" itself,
when it appeared in 1611.

In this he reminds his Most dread Sovereign "how convenient
it was, that out of the Original Sacred Tongues, together with
comparing of the laboures . . . of many worthy men who went
before us, there should be one more exact translation of the
Holy Scriptures into the *English Tongue*." The work of Wyclif,
Coverdale, and the Bishops was in fact visible and audible to
the Revisers as they sat at Oxford, Cambridge and Westminster;
and it is, no doubt, owing to this cause that the language and
rhythms of the Bible as we know it are in accord not with the
speech or taste of any one generation only, but with the essential
underlying character and genius of the nation. It is probable
that no book has ever so profoundly influenced the life and
literature of a whole race.

1612. Francis Beaumont (1586–1616) and John Fletcher (1579–1625)

BEAUMONT was a friend and disciple of Ben Jonson; JOHN
FLETCHER, his dramatic colleague, was nephew to Giles Fletcher
the Elder, and cousin to the Giles last above mentioned. Their
plays have many fine passages and some well-grounded plots;
but the situations are often worked up with morbid sentiment
and an excessive grossness. There is not enough common
human nature in them to ensure them any real survival; but
they still interest the antiquarians of the stage. On the other
hand the writers—or one of them—had an admirable sense of
humour, as may be seen by the piece of self-parody here extracted.
The Knight of the Burning Pestle (1612) remains delightfully
amusing to this day. It owes much to Cervantes, whose *Don
Quixote* had just been translated into English by Shelton.

1613. John Fletcher (1579–1625)

Of JOHN FLETCHER's songs it is enough to say that some of
them have been ascribed to Shakespeare, and that one at least

appears in *Twelfth Night*. Those who read Beddoes (*English Anthology*, p. 738) hear the last echo of this music.

1613. Samuel Purchas (1575?–1626)

Purchas continued the vast work of Hakluyt, with somewhat less distinction. The passage here given, and another in the same pages, suggested to Coleridge the famous fragmentary poem *Kubla Khan* (*English Anthology*, pp. 631–2). *Purchas His Pilgrimes* appeared in 1613.

1613–16. William Browne, of Tavistock (1588–1643)

This famous Epitaph, long believed to be Ben Jonson's, is now generally admitted to be by Browne. Professor Saintsbury, however, maintains that this " is entirely refuted by internal evidence." The same kind of evidence leads to the conjecture that Keats was familiar with Browne's longer works. The date 1613 is that of the first appearance of *Britannia's Pastorals*.

1615. George Wither (1588–1667)

This much praised and much imitated poem is said to have been written in the Marshalsea prison, to which Wither was committed in 1613 for publishing his satire *Abuses Stript and Whipt*. In the Civil War he took the side of the Parliament, and at the Restoration his verse fell, under the condemnation of Dryden, into undeserved but long-lasting contempt.

1616. George Chapman (1559–1634?)

Chapman as a dramatist was contemporary with Shakespeare: but his translation of Homer was not completed till 1616. The plays helped Dryden to some of his bombast: the *Homer* inspired Keats and drew from him a splendid sonnet. The passage from the *Iliad* VIII. here given may be compared with Tennyson's version of the same lines, which stands evidently in the same relation to Chapman's work as some of Turner's pictures to Claude's.

1621. Robert Burton (1577-1640)

Humour is largely represented in this English Anthology—as it ought to be. It may be said to be of five kinds. The first is that which is naturally incidental to any study of English social life: it is common to Chaucer's *Canterbury Tales*, his *Troilus and Criseyde*, and many of the great novels, such as *Tom Jones* and *Tristram Shandy*. Near to this is the more pointed satirical humour in *Richard the Redeless*, *Gossip Mine*, *Every Man in his Humour*, *Hudibras*, *The Way of the World*, *Gulliver's Travels*, Addison's *Essays*, *The Rape of the Lock*, Berkeley's *Essays* and passages like " The Dinner Party " in Cowper's poems. Deliberate, or instinctive, humour for its own sake is exemplified in Henryson's *Robin and Makyne*, Beaumont and Fletcher's *Knight of the Burning Pestle*, Suckling's poems, Gay's *Quidnunkies*, Sheridan's *Rivals*, Dickens's *Pickwick Papers*, and Meredith's *Egoist*. Simpler and more rollicking is the mood of *The Pilgrims' Sea Voyage* and *Saylors for my Money*. The fifth and most literary is the learned and whimsical humour of the connoisseur in human life. The earliest in this kind is Robert Burton; an occasional outburst in his letters brings Gray into the same class; and Lamb and Peacock are brilliant and accomplished members of it. But *The Anatomy of Melancholy* (1621) has given life to many more than can be here enumerated.

1623. William Drummond of Hawthornden (1585-1649)

DRUMMOND wrote imitative verse with occasional grace but more frequent stiffness. His prose is equally deliberate but much more successful: it might be described as the Euphuism of a more serious age, and it leads on to the far greater achievement of Sir Thomas Browne. *The Cypress Grove* was published in 1623.

1623. John Webster (?–1630?)

WEBSTER was a great poet and might possibly have been a great dramatist. If only certain fragments of his two most famous plays had survived, we should have placed him with Shakespeare and no other. As it is, his reputation has long outlasted his influence. The poignant and dazzling beauty of his lines is beyond all learning; and no one but Tourneur attempted to follow him to the extreme of inhuman cruelty and piled-up horror. Even in *The Duchess of Malfi* (1623) upon which his fame now rests, he forces his wonderful imagination to a complete break-down, attempting unnatural means and failing doubly to achieve the end of tragedy.

1624. Sir Henry Wotton (1568–1639)

WOTTON was an accomplished gentleman whose verse lives not so much by its poetical quality as by the charm and wit of its author expressed in forms of a classical tradition. *The Character of a Happy Life* descends from Martial, through Surrey's poem on the same theme (*English Anthology*, p. 121), and the line is not yet extinct. Written in looser verse, Wotton's reflections and compliments would probably have been forgotten in a month. In 1624 he retired from diplomacy to the Provostship of Eton, and his literary influence is dated from this period.

1625. Francis Quarles (1592–1644)

QUARLES wrote voluminously, and his *Emblems* (1634) had an immense success; but his popularity begins with his *Sion's Sonnets* in 1625. Coleridge read him with care, and the marginal annotations in his own copy show that he found life in him.

1627. Phineas Fletcher (1580–1650)

PHINEAS FLETCHER was the elder brother of the author of *Christ's Victory (ante)*, but as a poet he came out considerably later (1627). His poems, like his brother's, were of the Spenserian family, and known to Milton. More than this: it is plain that the passage here given from *The Apollyonists* contains the suggestion, and in some degree the inspiration, of the Satan of *Paradise Lost*. Scene, character, style and phrase form so obvious a parallel that if Fletcher's work had been published in 1672 instead of 1627 it would have been marked as a plagiarism.

1629. John Milton (I.) (1608–74)

MILTON's first period dates from the *Ode on the Nativity*, written in 1629, when he was twenty-one. His early work, Latin and English verse, shows him as " a gentle and sociable youth, a lover of music, gaiety, women, books, plays, and country pleasures: at the same time studious, religious, and high-minded: a temperament exceptionally happy." Then suddenly comes the great *Ode*, full of the natural magic " which takes common words and in some way beyond explanation makes of them a strange and memorable picture, a strange and haunting melody." Milton's own account of the writing of this poem is given in a Latin Elegy addressed by way of letter to his friend Diodati. After a playful passage on the connection of poetry with drinking, music, dancing and ladies' eyes, he tells of his new Ode, and gives the substance of it, compressed into three couplets made up of phrases whose English equivalents are easily recognisable.

L'ALLEGRO and IL PENSEROSO are of the same period, written shortly after Milton left Cambridge (1632) and while he was living in his father's country house at Horton in Buckinghamshire. They, too, show clearly that he was by birth far from Puritanism: his sense of beauty and his religious instinct were naturally at one; his mind had as yet no bitter or self-righteous habit.

1633. Fulke Greville, Lord Brooke (1554-1628)

FULKE GREVILLE was born in the same year as Philip Sidney and may have written his sonnets and songs as early; but they were not published till 1633, five years after his own death, and more than forty years after *Astrophel and Stella* first became famous. Greville's principal part during his life was that of a diplomatist, state official and wealthy peer; but he survives as the intimate friend, fellow poet, and biographer of Sidney.

1633. George Herbert (1593-1632)

GEORGE HERBERT died at 39, and his poems were published in the following year (1633). His influence has been great and lasting, but most of his followers (Keble the best of them) have resembled him rather in piety than in originality.

1633. John Ford (1586-1639)

FORD is admitted to be the best of the Jacobean dramatists, and *The Broken Heart* (1633), one of his two best plays, has been revived for a few nights within living memory. But it is no longer easy to find an audience for plays whose strongest situations are obviously impossible ones. The climax of *The Broken Heart*, here given, is not merely imitation but a parody of drama: and the would-be great emotional scene in which the heroine, smitten by successive messages of disaster, calmly goes on with her ceremonial dance, is, when compared with genuine tragedy, an equally hollow show. For the sake of such an effect Ford will sacrifice the breadth of view, sanity, and truth to human nature, which give dramatic fitness and a lasting power over the emotions.

1635. Martin Parker (c. 1635)

This splendid song has reappeared in many versions or adaptations, of which the one beginning "Ye Gentlemen of England" was the best known until eclipsed by Campbell's "Ye Mariners of England"—a daring but entirely justifiable transformation. But the original remains the best—genius blows through it in a gale without a lull.

For the date 1635 see Sir Charles Firth's *Naval Songs and Ballads*.

1637. Sir William Davenant (1606–68)

DAVENANT was a Royalist poet and playwright who succeeded Ben Jonson as Laureate (1637), was rescued from Puritans in the Civil War by Milton and was later a friend of Dryden. He survives in this one song of the courtly tradition.

1638. Sir John Suckling (1609–42)

SUCKLING was a Cavalier poet with the traditional charm; but to this was added a gift of unusually exquisite humour. His collected poems and plays were published after his death, but in 1638 appeared *Aglaura*, from which the song "Why so pale and wan, fond lover?" is taken.

1640. Thomas Carew (1595?–1639?)

CAREW wrote a masque under the influence of Ben Jonson (1634), but his poems were not published till (1640) after his death. Seven or eight of them are of the finest poetry of his age; "Ask me no more" is one of those magical pieces of supremely artful simplicity where, as in Shakespeare's "Fear no more the heat of the sun," the sound and not the sense appears to give the meaning.

1642. Sir Thomas Browne (1605–82)

SIR THOMAS BROWNE's influence dates from the publication of his first and most popular book, *Religio Medici*, in 1642: the *Christian Morals* was written later, perhaps not finally revised, and only published (1716) long after his death. But if it lacks anything of the grave humour, the continually surprising quaintness and exquisitely carven phrasing of the *Religio*, it gains by a more evident sincerity, and its philosophy is not less profound for being more easily intelligible.

1644. John Milton (II.) (1608–74)

MILTON in his second period was an entirely changed man. The young and happy poet, the courtly gentleman and æsthetic churchman had disappeared, and in his place there had entered a strenuous and almost lawless controversialist, a Parliamentarian, and official of the Commonwealth. He wrote in prose—loftily and sonorously for Liberty of Unlicens'd Printing (*Areopagitica*, 1644), furiously and scurrilously for Freedom of Divorce (*English Anthology*, pp. 344, 347). How far the transformation had gone is shown even more strikingly by a passage in the tract " against Prelaty." There, between fierce strokes at the " inquisitorious and tyrannical duncery " of bishops, and the writing of the " vulgar Amorist " or " riming Parasite " of the Royalist party, he thrusts in an autobiographical paragraph of the greatest interest (*English Anthology*, p. 346), a kind of prospectus of *Paradise Lost*, not free from ostentation and self-consciousness even in its eloquent piety; but when we remember the chances of the time and the eventual issue, one of the highest challenges ever thrown down to human fate.

1645. Edmund Waller (1606–87)

WALLER was neither a great man nor a great poet, but these two pieces the English world has not been willing to let die.
The first edition of his poems is dated 1645.

1646. James Shirley (1596–1666)

SHIRLEY is the last poet who was an Elizabethan born. For forty years he wrote plays which have long been mere names, and he lived to be called dull by Dryden after the Restoration. But he wrote this one poem which has never faded.
His collected poems appeared in 1646.

1646. Richard Crashaw (1613?–49)

CRASHAW, the son of a Puritan clergyman, is one of the few English poets in the last four centuries who have belonged to the unreformed religion. (See note on the Coverdale Bible, 1535.) He is more definitely inspired at one moment and uninspired at another, than any writer in our collection. He has a music and an intensity of religious imagination which have given him an immense influence; but a considerable part of his verse has long since died stifled by its own tawdry verbiage.
His *Steps to the Temple* and *Delights of the Muses* appeared in one volume, in 1646.

1647. Abraham Cowley (1618–67)

COWLEY was a scholar and a man of great ability and personal charm: a prosaic age mistook him early in his career for a great poet. His fame dates from 1647 when he published the lyrical collection called *The Mistress: or Several Copies of Love Verses.*

Passion is wholly absent from them, but there are some pleasing pieces, of which *The Wish* is perhaps the best. It is either the source or the amplification of a phrase in a letter of his own, also quoted here. Cowley's prose, especially that in his *Essays* (1668), is better than his verse; but it was to his verse that he owed his influence. His celebrated *Pindaric Odes* introduced a fashion which for fifty years afterwards led his followers away from sincerity of expression. But they also made possible some of the finest work of Dryden, Gray, Collins, Wordsworth, Shelley and Tennyson.

It has sometimes been thought that Milton may have taken a suggestion for his Great Consult in Hell from the opening of Cowley's *Davideis*, a sacred epic written for the most part while Cowley was "a young student at Cambridge," and therefore some years before Milton's "prospectus" of *Paradise Lost* (see above under date 1644). But the resemblance is slight; and Milton, who was the elder by ten years, was probably familiar long before this with Phineas Fletcher's much more congenial poem (see above, 1627). The real interest of the *Davideis* lies in its use of rhymed couplets, often pithy but more often grotesquely absurd, which point with startling directness to the flattest levels of the school of Dryden, many years ahead.

1648. Robert Herrick (1591–1674)

HERRICK was two men, of whom only one has survived. The one who died was an imitator of Martial in his trivial and coarse vein, and of Ben Jonson at his offensive moments. The other, the Herrick of the *Noble Numbers* and the *Hesperides* (1648), has a place by himself in English literature, as the writer of the largest collection of the most exquisite poems. Of these some have, like Campion's best, a peculiar "singable" quality, and were perfectly set by Henry Lawes and others; but the most of them have the music of poetry, a music which belongs to themselves and is " the sound of the meaning " and not suggestive of any singing voice or instrument.

Like Carew, the only poet with whom he can be grouped, Herrick suffered a long eclipse behind the clouds of political disturbance. His reputation only shone out again two centuries afterwards, and may possibly, in an age of even greater chaos, survive to correct current misunderstandings of the meaning of form in art.

1649. Sir Richard Lovelace (1618–58)

LOVELACE, the typical Cavalier poet, published his volume, *Lucasta*, in 1649. His best poems, like the man himself, were to his own time " incomparably graceful," and English chivalry, " going to the wars " has ever since gone in the remembrance of them.

1650. Henry Vaughan (1621–95)

VAUGHAN " the Silurist " (South Welshman) published his volume *Silex Scintillans* in 1650, *Olor Iscanus* in 1651. He was a confessed follower of George Herbert, whom he far surpasses (when at his best) in depth of thought and feeling, as well as in intensity of expression.

1650. Edward Hyde, Earl of Clarendon (1608–1674)

CLARENDON's History of the Great Rebellion was not published till 1704, when he had been dead thirty years. But the book was begun in 1646 and is a political record: his influence may well be dated from 1650, when the death of Charles I. had left him in the position of chief minister of the Royalist party in exile. His History is lengthy and untidily written, but vivid and well conceived; as a gallery of contemporary portraits it is unsurpassed; and this of Cromwell is perhaps the best. The frank partisanship of the last sentence only sets off the " wonderful civility, generosity and bounty " of the whole picture.

1652. Thomas Hobbes (1588–1679)

HOBBES was actually the last of the Elizabethans: he was born in the year of the Armada (1588) and died in 1679. His masterpiece, the famous *Leviathan*, did not appear till 1652, when he was already 64, and had wasted time on mathematical books of no repute, and a verse translation of Homer. His style is reminiscent of the prose of Bacon and Ben Jonson; but its combined vitality, clearness, and rigid terseness are his own contribution to scientific literature and have had a lasting effect.

1652. Andrew Marvell (1621–78)

MARVELL's living poems were nearly all written between 1650 and 1652. Up to this time he had been a friend of Lovelace and an admirer of Charles I. In 1653 he was proposed by Milton as his coadjutor in the Latin Secretaryship to the Commonwealth, and the appointment was made in 1657. He followed Milton in becoming a fierce politician; sat in the Roundhead Parliament, and held his seat after the Restoration, as a member of the Opposition. His very beautiful poems range from the Cavalier piece " To his Coy Mistress " to the Puritan " Bermudas," and are thereby peculiarly characteristic of the " two-mindedness " of the modern Englishman.

1654. Sir William Temple (1628–99)

1654. Dorothy Osborne (married 1654, died 1695)

TEMPLE, of a Parliamentarian family, fell in love in 1647 with Dorothy Osborne, daughter of the Royalist Governor of Guernsey, and married her in 1654 after bitter opposition. His letters and essays are a distinguished influence in English life, and though they were not published till long after his death their effect was felt much earlier. He had a great position as confidential adviser to William III., and Swift and Esther Johnson (Stella) were both inmates of his house.

DOROTHY OSBORNE lives by the charm of her letters, and one of the most delightful of them, written not long before her marriage, is here placed side by side with her lover's most famous pages, though the actual date of the latter is not ascertainable.

1656. Jeremy Taylor (1613–67)

JEREMY TAYLOR was during his most fertile period a Royalist living alternately in a Parliament prison and in retirement in Wales under the protection of the Earl of Carbery. His influence may be supposed to have reached its full force by 1656, by which time he had published his *Liberty of Prophesying, Holy Living, Holy Dying,* and *A Discourse of Friendship* (1656), and could venture to return to a London congregation. He was a splendid orator, often too full of fancy to please his contemporaries; but his mind was simple and gentle, and he had the great merit of being " the earliest great divine to free himself completely from the subtleties and spinosities of the Schools " (Gosse).

1656. Thomas Fuller (1608–61)

FULLER'S huge *Church History of Britain* (1656) is his greatest work; but *The Worthies of England,* published after his death, is equally voluminous and perhaps even more characteristic of him. He was a great Englishman, and loved his country's earth almost as much as her people and her fame.

1657. Richard Baxter (1615–91)

BAXTER was a non-conforming clergyman, persecuted by Charles II. and James II., and insulted by Judge Jeffreys. His *Saint's Everlasting Rest* (1650) and *Call to the Unconverted* (1657) have had an immense influence on many generations, and were textbooks of the great Evangelical revival of the nineteenth century.

1657. Henry King, Bishop of Chichester (1592–1669)

BISHOP KING was, like Hobbes, a late Elizabethan, but died ten years before him. He was the friend of Ben Jonson, and of Donne whose poetical disciple he was. He lacked Donne's intensity and originality, but a grave and tender note gives him a beauty of his own. It is hardly to be doubted that Tennyson when he wrote his *Love and Duty* was matching his own art against King's *Renunciation*; and if so the verdict must go in favour of the Cavalier bishop. King's poems were published in 1657.

1660–70. John Wilmot, Earl of Rochester (1648–1680)

ROCHESTER was the type of all that was worst and wittiest among the rakes of the Revolution; but between 1660 and 1670 he wrote a few excellent songs, of which *Return* is both touching and memorable.

1663. Samuel Butler (1612–80)

In 1663 was published the first part of *Hudibras, Written in the Time of the Late Wars*; in 1664 the second part, and the conclusion in 1678. It is the most characteristically English of satires and perhaps the most successful, being at once entirely personal and sincere, and entirely representative of the national feeling of reaction. Its modernity, the concentration of its scornful energy, and the inexhaustible humour of its rhymes and rhythms, are more than enough to explain its immense popularity and lasting fame.

1664. Samuel Pepys (1633–1703)

PEPYS' *Diary* was not published till 120 years after his death; the extract here given is placed at the date of the events recorded, as a historical document (like *The Paston Letters*). But it belongs to literature, in a very unusual but undeniable fashion. The writer has the gift of confession carried to the point of genius: he confesses the truth, the whole truth and nothing but the truth—and yet not objectively, but in a style invariably marked with the stamp of a unique personality.

1665. Izaak Walton (1593–1683)

WALTON'S *Compleat Angler* was printed in 1653 and revised in 1655—a book of " infantile grace " rather than of conscious literary art. (Andrew Lang said of him " Heaven meant him for the place he fills, as it meant the cowslip and the mayfly.") But his real influence in literature dates from 1665, when he began publishing his famous *Lives*—first that of Richard Hooker, and afterwards those of Donne, George Herbert and Sanderson, with the memoir of Wotton already printed in his *Reliquiæ Wottonianæ* (1651).

1668. Sir Charles Sedley (1639–1701)

SEDLEY'S literary reputation was made by *The Mulberry Garden*, a comedy, in 1668, but he is remembered for two songs, this one *To Celia* and " Phyllis is my only joy."

1670. Thomas Traherne (1636?–1674)

TRAHERNE'S poems were discovered in MS. and published by Mr. Bertram Dobell in 1903, with some extracts from another MS., entitled *Centuries of Meditations*. The poems appear to have been written for the most part in early life, and the *Meditations* between 1667 and 1674 when Traherne was living in the house of Sir Orlando Bridgeman as chaplain; publishing his controversial work *Roman Forgeries*, and preparing his *Christian Ethicks* for the press. The approximate date 1670 has therefore been assigned to him here; but it must be borne in mind that the prose extract is not the original of the poem *Wonder* but an expanded version, or meditation upon it. Both the prose and verse are strongly influenced by Vaughan.

1671. John Milton (III.)

MILTON began to write *Paradise Lost* in 1657, after some years of preparation, and it was published ten years later; *Paradise Regained* followed in 1671. This date marks, no doubt, the completion of the achievement to which Fame will always point; but we have already seen that Milton's poetical power was supreme from his early youth. The influence of his third period has been greater but less favourable: his Latinism threatened to petrify the diction of English poetry. Of all his successors Robert Bridges alone has been able to wear the Miltonic dignity without ill coming of it. *Samson Agonistes* has been far less known, but is perhaps a greater poem than *Paradise Lost*. It has been read lately by a generation smitten with the just but unhappy anger of war, and desiring at one and the same time to be, like the blind Giant, "on his enemies fully revenged" and to have "peace and consolation . . . And calm of mind, all passion spent."

1678. John Bunyan (1628–88)

BUNYAN, the third, with Langland and Spenser, of the great English allegorists, published his *Pilgrim's Progress* (the First Part) in 1678. It has been said to owe something to a *Pélérinage de l'Ame Humaine*, though Bunyan could hardly have read this. What is not doubtful is that he had read the Authorised Version of the Bible and without conscious art had acquired a style familiar and dignified, fit to express his extraordinary sincerity, wit and insight. His verse is equally a wonder: nothing could be better than his preface "to his Reader" in rhymed couplets; and his Shepherd Boy's song in the Valley of Humiliation is a hymn as perfect as the finest songs of the Cavaliers.

1681. John Dryden (1631–1700)

DRYDEN was 50 when he published in November 1681 the first part of *Absalom and Achitophel*, followed in March 1682 by *The Medal*, in October by *Mac Flecknoe*, and in November by the second part of *Absalom and Achitophel*. With these brilliant satires his fame and power began. In 1697 he wrote his great ode *Alexander's Feast*, and in 1699 included it in a volume of *Fables* adapted from Chaucer and Boccaccio. His critical Essay on Chaucer is a masterpiece worthy to introduce *The Canterbury Tales*; his judgments on his contemporaries are quoted to this day. He made in 1664 a famous reference to " Shakespeare, who, with some errors not to be avoyded in that Age, had undoubtedly a larger Soul of Poesie than ever any of our Nation." His influence in the world of his time was immense; its decay and the obsolescence of most of his work is due to his too great reliance on rhetoric, and to his prosaic outlook and preoccupation: whether this was forced by him on his age or by the age on him is matter of dispute.

1685. George Savile, Marquess of Halifax (1630–95)

HALIFAX was a successful politician whose literary reputation rests on his treatises, the most celebrated and memorable of which is *The Character of a Trimmer*, written and circulated in MS. in 1684–5 and printed anonymously with others three years afterwards.

1688. John Evelyn (1620–1706)

EVELYN was thirteen years older than Pepys, whom he patronised, but he had not a tenth part of his influence or a hundredth part of his genius and subsequent fame. Here his *Diary*, like that of Pepys, is treated as a document of social history, and the extract from it is placed by the date of the events which it records.

1690. John Locke (1632–1704)

LOCKE'S *Essay Concerning Human Understanding* appeared in 1690. According to one judge, " to give a just idea of the influence of Locke it would be necessary to write the history of philosophy from his time to our own." According to another, the " obstinate Philistinism of thought and expression " which is the besetting sin of the eighteenth century, was due to him more than to any other. He remains an easy and agreeable writer.

1700. William Congreve (1670–1729)

CONGREVE—a young gentleman of 23 befriended by Dryden —gained his first success with his play *The Old Bachelor* (1693), and reached the height of his literary power in *The Way of the World* (1700), though it was at the moment so little approved that he abandoned the stage. It is a world of almost tragic imagination, with brilliant pictures from the " real world " inwoven. For Dryden's estimate see above (*English Anthology*, p. 428).

1705. Isaac Watts (1674–1748)

WATTS published his famous hymns—*Horæ Lyricæ*—in 1705, and his *Psalms of David* in 1719.

1709. Sir Richard Steele (1672–1729)

In 1707 STEELE, who had failed as a dramatist, was appointed by Harley, the Tory leader, to the important post of Gazetteer. In the same year he married his " Dear Prue," a beautiful Welsh lady of some property. To her he wrote the famous letters of which a selection is here given: letters " as good as a play," acted by a rebellious, bibulous, adoring and yielding husband and the " tormenting peevish beauty " who fought and won " full power " as his absolute " governor."

In 1709 Steele began to issue *The Tatler*, which ran till 1711 and was succeeded by *The Spectator*, produced in alliance with Addison; *The Guardian* followed in 1713. In 1715 he was knighted and entered the House of Commons.

1710. Jonathan Swift (1667–1745)

In 1710 Swift, who had first been secretary to Sir William Temple, then " hedge-parson " and Whig pamphleteer, went over to the Tories and was very favourably received by Harley; he made his reputation immediately in the Tory *Examiner* and began in 1711 his *Journal to Stella*. The *Tale of a Tub* had been published anonymously in 1704, and *Gulliver's Travels* appeared in 1726. Each of these has been called " the greatest book of the century."

The simultaneous letters from Swift to Pope and from Gay to Swift show the method of concealment practised by Swift upon his literary intimates, and the foredoomed futility of it. Scott with *Waverley* was less subtle and more successful.

1711. Joseph Addison (1672–1719)

In 1711 Addison, who had helped Steele in *The Tatler*, joined him in founding *The Spectator*. In this he brought to perfection the type of essay originated by Steele. " Whoever wishes to attain an English style, familiar but not coarse, and elegant but not ostentatious, must give his days and nights to the volumes of Addison " (Dr. Johnson). But he would give them in vain if he had not the temper of the man—Addison's prose and verse, though without imagination, are the expression of an exquisite kindness and sincerity.

1712. Alexander Pope (1688-1734)

THE RAPE OF THE LOCK was published in Lintot's *Miscellany* (1712) in the form here given: two years later it reappeared with the addition of an elaborate machinery of gnomes and sylphs. As to the effect of this opinion differs strongly; the simpler original pleased Addison, and " lifted Pope at once to the first rank of living European poets." Swift in the year following said that " the best poet in England was Mr. Pope." He continued to earn the title anew with his *Homer* (1715) *Dunciad* (1725) and *Essay on Man* (1733-4).

It has been often debated whether Pope's verse is poetry. In the Introduction to the *Essay on Man* he himself says: " This I might have done in prose, but I chose verse, and even rhyme, for two reasons: the one . . . that principles, maxims, or precepts, so written, both strike the reader more strongly at first, and are more easily retained. The other . . . I found I could express them more *shortly* this way than in prose itself; and . . . much of the *force* as well as *grace* of argument or instructions depends on their *conciseness*." This is clear, and final; but a little poetry has crept in, and *The Rape of the Lock* is a complete poetical creation.

The letters here given illustrate Pope's wit (which does not spare even the Roman Church), his relations with Steele and *The Spectator*, and his own pathetic consciousness of his bodily deformity (*English Anthology*, p. 477).

1713. John Gay (1685-1732)

GAY entered the literary society of London in 1711 as the friend and protégé of Steele and Pope. His *Rural Sports* had a success in 1713, *The Shepherd's Week* in 1714, *The What d'ye Call It* in 1715, his *Fables* in 1727, *The Beggar's Opera* in 1728 and *Polly* in 1729.   The immense popularity of *The Beggar's Opera* has held good to the present day; in 1728 it was regarded as an attack on the Italian Opera and even on the Court. *Polly* was forbidden the stage, and appeared as a private publication and a wider scandal. The two shorter poems here given are perfect examples of Gay's wit and versatility.

1713.   Bishop George Berkeley (1685–1753)

BERKELEY came from Ireland to London in 1713, in order to publish his *Dialogues between Hylas and Philonous* (Matter and Mind). He became the intimate friend of Steele, Swift, Addison and Pope, and was loved by all for his character, charm, intellectual distinction, and " every virtue under Heaven " (Pope). His style is as flawless as Addison's; it is the expression of an equally urbane temper, with more personal flavour.

1718.   Matthew Prior (1664–1721)

PRIOR, after being for years in high place as a Tory Under-Secretary of State and Ambassador, was impeached and imprisoned. At his release in 1717 his poems were collected, and they were published by subscription in 1718.

1718.   Lady Mary Wortley Montagu (1689–1762)

LADY MARY WORTLEY MONTAGU, the friend of Addison, Steele, Congreve and (for a time) Pope, left England for Constantinople in 1716, and in the following two years wrote some of the best of her famous letters, including the one here quoted.

1719. Daniel Defoe (1659–1731)

DEFOE was a controversial journalist who suddenly invented in his sixtieth year an entirely new kind of romance: *Robinson Crusoe* (1719). His other memorable books were *Moll Flanders* and *The History of the Plague* (both in 1722), and *Roxana* in 1724. The fame of *Robinson Crusoe* is world-wide, and its detailed realistic method has influenced many—notably R. L. Stevenson.

1726. James Thomson (1700–48)

THOMSON came to London from Scotland in 1725 to make his fortune, and made it in 1726 by the publication of his poem *Winter*, followed by the other *Seasons*, *Summer* (1727), *Spring* (1728) and *Autumn* (1730). Their merit and great popularity formed for the remainder of the century a chief bulwark of the poetical against the encroachment of the prosaic in verse. The rhythm of his blank verse is frequently reproduced by Tennyson.

1726. Bishop Joseph Butler (1692–1752)

BISHOP BUTLER'S position as a philosophical divine was secured by the publication in 1726 of *Fifteen Sermons*. In 1736 the *Analogy of Religion* appeared, and in 1738 he became Bishop of Bristol.

1735. Henry St. John, Viscount Bolingbroke (1678–1751)

BOLINGBROKE'S career was that of a politician and orator. His book *A Dissertation on Parties* appeared in 1735, and *The Idea of a Patriot King*, though undated, is assigned to the same date.

1739–40. Samuel Richardson (1689–1761)

In 1739 RICHARDSON attracted the attention of some publishers, who engaged him to write a set of *Familiar Letters* as a popular handbook. From this root sprang in 1740–1 *Pamela: or Virtue Rewarded*, the first English " novel of manners." *Clarissa: or the History of a Young Lady* (1747–8) and *Sir Charles Grandison* (1754) achieved an incredible popularity.

1739. Samuel Johnson (1709–84)

JOHNSON came to London with Garrick in 1737: in 1738 he published his poem *London*, which was successful enough to attract Pope's favourable notice, and by 1739 Johnson was on the staff of *The Gentleman's Magazine*. The *Plan of a Dictionary* was issued in 1747, and *The Vanity of Human Wishes* appeared in 1749. In the same year *Irene*, a tragedy which had been refused in 1738, was successfully produced by Garrick at Drury Lane. The Dictionary was finished in 1754; *The Idler* begun in 1758; *Rasselas* appeared in 1759; Johnson's *Shakespeare* in 1765; and his *Lives of the Poets* in 1781.

In 1763 he began to be attended by Boswell: in 1764 he founded, with a group of friends, the literary society called " The Club," which has lasted to the present day. It was suggested to him by Sir Joshua Reynolds, and among other original members were Edmund Burke and Oliver Goldsmith.

The power of Johnson's character and conversation were so great that his influence may reasonably be dated not from his earliest success but from his entry into the world of letters.

For a counter-attack on his autocratic judgments see the letters by Cowper (*English Anthology*, pp. 572–4).

1739. David Hume (1711–76)

HUME's first work, the *Treatise of Human Nature*, was written 1734–7 in France, but not published till 1739; and his *Essays*,

Moral and Political, appeared in 1742 anonymously. But he was already known and highly estimated by Butler and Adam Smith.

1742. Henry Fielding (1707–54)

PAGE

The Broken Arm (*The History of Tom Jones*) . . 516

In 1742 FIELDING published *Joseph Andrews* as an ironical parallel to Richardson's *Pamela*—the virtuous footman beside the virtuous lady's maid. This enraged Richardson, but in 1749 the appearance of *Tom Jones* inflicted a far more fatal comparison upon him. This time Cervantes was Fielding's model, and the result was, if not the first English novel, certainly the first Englishman's novel.

1747–85. Horace Walpole, Earl of Orford (1717–97)

War and Waste (*Memoirs of the Reign of King George II.*) 521

To the Countess of Upper Ossory . . . 523

HORACE WALPOLE during his life was a virtuoso and a personage rather than a literary man; but he was an admirable letter-writer and amateur chronicler, from 1747 to 1785.

1748. Tobias Smollett (1721–71)

Tom Bowling (*Roderick Random*) . . . 524

SMOLLETT was a surgeon's mate in the navy, and afterwards a surgeon at Westminster. After failing in satirical poetry he achieved success in 1748 with *Roderick Random*, a novel in imitation of *Don Quixote* and *Gil Blas*. *Peregrine Pickle* followed in 1751, and *Humphrey Clinker*, Sir Walter Scott's favourite, in 1771.

For a descendant and namesake of Tom Bowling, see Dibdin (*English Anthology*, p. 599).

1751. Thomas Gray (1716–71)

Elegy written in a Country Churchyard . . 527

To Dr. Clarke 531

To Mr. Nicholls 532

GRAY, a very early friend of Horace Walpole, wrote poems from 1742, but his famous *Elegy* was published in 1751, as a separate quarto, and reprinted in a volume of collected poems in 1753. It had many imitators—William Whitehead's *Elegies* are better than any intentional parody—and some detractors, including Mrs. Meynell; but it remains one of the most famous poems in the language.

Gray was one of our best letter-writers: in the first of those here given he anticipates the flavour of Charles Lamb; in the second he paints the first sunset in English.

1746. William Collins (1721–59)

PAGE

Ode to Evening   534
How sleep the Brave   536

COLLINS came to London in 1745, and in 1746, when aged 25, published his little volume of *Odes*. It was unsuccessful, and he burnt the edition. It contained at least five poems of incomparable beauty and destined him to fill one of the highest niches of Fame.

1760. James MacPherson (1736–96)

Ossian's Farewell (*The War of Caros—Poems of Ossian*)   536

In 1760 MACPHERSON published anonymously *Fragments of Ancient Gaelic Poetry*, and in 1762 *Fingal*, an epic professing to be translated from Ossian. If not this, it may have been a deliberate forgery, or a concoction from genuine relics. Johnson denounced it; Gray was puzzled but inclined to belief (see letter, *English Anthology*, p. 532); Walpole was contemptuously indifferent (see letter, *English Anthology*, p. 524). Meanwhile MacPherson made a fortune in Florida and India, got into Parliament, and was eventually buried in Westminster Abbey.

1760. Laurence Sterne (1713–68)

Widow Wadman and my Uncle Toby (*Tristram Shandy*)   538

The Reverend LAURENCE STERNE had the first volumes of his *Tristram Shandy* printed at York in 1759, and in 1760 took them to London to be published. Garrick had already talked enthusiastically of the book, and Sterne was instantly the fashion. He finished Vols. V. and VI. in 1761 and went to France for his health; Vol. IX. was published in 1767; *cetera desunt*.

D

1763. Christopher Smart (1722–70)

SMART, a scholar and fellow of Pembroke College, Oxford, became insane at the age of twenty-nine, and twelve years later (1763) wrote in the asylum at Bedlam his one poem, *The Song to David*. It is a breathless rhapsody, and was unique until 1913, when Mr. Ralph Hodgson's *Song of Honour* appeared—a singular instance of one masterpiece directly inspiring another of equal beauty and originality.

1766. Oliver Goldsmith (1728–74)

In 1762 Johnson pronounced GOLDSMITH to be " one of the first men we now have as an author," and sold for him his novel, *The Vicar of Wakefield*, which appeared at last in 1766 and made his name at once. In 1767 he made £500 by his comedy *The Good-Natur'd Man*; in 1770 appeared his much-quoted poem *The Deserted Village*. It was dedicated, in the charming letter here given with it, to his friend and fellow-member of " The Club," Sir Joshua Reynolds.

1769. Thomas Chatterton (1752–70)

In 1758, when he was under 16, CHATTERTON produced the forged " Rowley Papers " and quasi-fifteenth-century poems. He sent them to Walpole, and Walpole handed them on to Gray, who immediately pronounced against their authenticity. In 1769 Chatterton came to London and sold his *Revenge*, a musical farce, for £5; but in 1770 poisoned himself to avoid death by starvation. His poems are in parts beautiful, but his fame is in reality a kind of charitable subscription, called forth by sympathy for his miserable life and his " desperate appeal to the romantic past " from the cold conventionality of his time.

1769. Sir Joshua Reynolds (1723–92)

REYNOLDS was unanimously elected first President of the Royal Academy in 1768 and delivered the first of his celebrated *Discourses* in 1769. For his literary friendships see the notes on Johnson and Goldsmith, *supra*.

1770. Edmund Burke (1729–97)

BURKE's brilliant career opened in 1770 with the anonymous publication of his *Thoughts on the Causes of the Present Discontents*, at first attributed to Junius. His immense popularity was not gained by his fine pamphlets on American affairs (1774–5), but by his *Reflections on the Revolution in France* (1790) and his *Thoughts on the Prospect of a Regicide Peace* (1795). The striking parallel between the European situation in his age and in ours has been vehemently made to prove both the value and the futility of arguments drawn from historical examples.

(1774). Philip Dormer Stanhope, Earl of Chesterfield (1694–1773)

CHESTERFIELD's *Letters to his Son*, published (1774) after his death, are his title to literary fame, though he had also written a few excellent political essays.

1775. Richard Brinsley Sheridan (1751–1816)

SHERIDAN's literary career began and ended with *The Rivals* (1775), *The School for Scandal* (1777) and *The Critic* (1779), all produced when he was between 24 and 28.

1776. Edward Gibbon (1737–94)

GIBBON's *Decline and Fall of the Roman Empire* was planned in 1764, and begun in 1770. The first volume, finished in 1773, was published in 1776, and had a resounding success in London and Paris. The whole book was finished in 1787, and publication was completed in 1788.

1778. Frances Burney (1752–1848)

FANNY BURNEY (Madame d'Arblay) was the daughter of Dr. Charles Burney, a friend of Johnson, Burke and Reynolds, and a member of " The Club." Her novels, *Evelina* (1778) and *Cecilia* (1782), made her famous though her name did not appear on them, and she received the appointment of Second Keeper of the Robes to Queen Charlotte. Her entertaining *Diary* was published (1842–6) after her death.

1781. Jeremy Bentham (1748–1832)

BENTHAM'S *Fragment on Government*, published anonymously in 1776, when he was only 28, was at first attributed to Lord Mansfield, and gained for its author the friendship and interest of Lord Shelburne and the Whigs. For four years he was a constant inmate of Bowood, and by 1781 had reached a position of great importance both in the public view and in his own. His *Introduction to the Principles of Morals and Legislation*, written and printed in 1780 but unpublished till 1789, contains " the bedrock of his philosophy," and Professor Elton in his *Survey of English Literature* also comments on the linguistic experiments in Bentham's later works, which gave us such words as " international," " codify " and " minimise."

1785. William Cowper (1731–1800)

COWPER'S first *Poems* (including *Table Talk*) were published in 1782. His *John Gilpin* appeared anonymously in 1783, and in 1785 *The Task* achieved a great success. His " incomparably witty, tender and graceful *Letters*," as Mr. Gosse has well called them, were published in 1803, after his death. The two here are selected for the interest of their comments on the poems of Milton, Prior and Dryden, and their *Lives* by Johnson (" King Critic ").

1786. Robert Burns (1759–96)

BURNS published in July 1786 his immortal *Poems, chiefly in the Scottish Dialect*, and with them " the reserve and quietism of the eighteenth century broke up."

> O ye douce folk, that live by rule,
> Grave, tideless-blooded, calm, and cool,
> Compar'd wi' you—O fool! fool! fool!
> How much unlike!
> Your hearts are just a standing pool,
> Your lives, a dyke!
> (*English Anthology*, pp. 578–83.)

1787. William Blake (1757–1827)

BLAKE engraved and published his *Songs of Innocence* in 1787, *The Book of Thel* in 1789, and *The Marriage of Heaven and Hell* in 1790. In 1794 he published in the ordinary manner his *Songs of Experience* and several of his prophetic books. In 1804 he engraved his *Jerusalem* and *Milton*. Lamb first heard of him in 1824 (see *English Anthology*, pp. 664–5). Blake's poetry is the work of one deeply read in Chaucer, the Bible, the Elizabethans and Ossian, and in the spirit of these he sang out of sight and hearing of the classical age. But his deepest inspiration came from within himself; his poetry has a timeless quality which belongs only to the greatest. The separate but

simultaneous appearance of Burns and Blake was the most
portentous conjunction ever seen in the poetic sky. Of Blake's
many followers W. B. Yeats and Mary Coleridge are the most
remarkable (see *post*, p. 85).

1789. Gilbert White (1720–93)

GILBERT WHITE wrote *The Natural History and Antiquities
of Selborne* between 1780 and 1788 and published it in 1789.
It was the first book of its kind in English, and is still a classic
both of science and literature.

1791. James Boswell (1740–95)

BOSWELL came to London in 1760, but did not succeed in
meeting Johnson till " Monday the 16th of May " 1763, as
here related. He then travelled; on his return in 1768 he began
his unique collection of notes for *The Life of Dr. Johnson*, which
he published in 1791: the most minute, fascinating and famous
biography ever written, and the work of a man who had at
least " a genius."

1798. Charles Dibdin (1745–1814)

DIBDIN's first song, *Blow High, Blow Low*, was produced about
1776, and he wrote till 1810. He reached his greatest popularity
and patriotic influence during the wars of 1793–8—the period
of " the First of June," St. Vincent, Camperdown and the
Nile. His exemplars were Martin Parker and Gay. For the
name *Tom Bowling* see Smollett, *ante* (1748).

1798. William Wordsworth (1770–1850)

WORDSWORTH was living at Alfoxden, and Coleridge at Nether Stowey in close intimacy with him, when in 1798 they published their famous and epoch-making volume of Lyrical Ballads : see Hazlitt's very interesting account of them (*English Anthology*, pp. 741–5). Wordsworth the same year left for Germany and there began *The Prelude*, which was not published till after his death in 1850. In 1802 he married Mary Hutchinson, and in 1803 travelled with her and his inseparable sister Dorothy through the Highlands; *The Solitary Reaper* belongs to this episode. *The Happy Warrior* in 1805 commemorates Nelson, and in some degree his own brother Captain John Wordsworth, lost at sea. In 1812 he moved to the Lake country, where he wrote *The Excursion* in 1814, and the *Sonnets to the River Duddon* in 1820. In 1831 he visited Scott at Abbotsford, and in 1843 he became Poet Laureate. The Preface to the second edition of the *Lyrical Ballads* (1800) places Wordsworth in the highest rank of English literary critics.

1798. Samuel Taylor Coleridge (1772–1834)

COLERIDGE was two years younger than Wordsworth and was attracted to the poetical partnership by reading the first fragment of *The Excursion* in 1797. His contribution to the *Lyrical Ballads* consisted of only four poems to Wordsworth's nineteen, but included *The Rime of the Ancyent Marinere*, which in originality and beauty as well as in length eclipsed all the rest. In 1798 he began *Christabel* (which has an important Preface on the use of stress in English verse) and wrote the fragment *Kubla Khan*. By these poems he proved himself, though weaker than Wordsworth in purpose, dignity and moral power, a greater master of metre and of magical charm. Together they brought the clear light of day back to English poets, long straitened and stifled by the stony monuments built by themselves and their predecessors of the Augustan age. For the origin of *Kubla Khan* see note on Purchas (1613, *English Anthology*, p. 294), and for Lamb's view of it see the letter to Wordsworth, *English Anthology*, p. 663 (" an owl that won't bear daylight ").

1799. Thomas Campbell (1777–1844)

In 1799 CAMPBELL published at Edinburgh his *Pleasures of Hope,* and " the demand for copies was unprecedented "; Scott's friendship followed immediately, and general recognition. *Hohenlinden* was written in 1800; *The Battle of the Baltic* (1801) appeared in its present much revised form in 1804; *Gertrude of Wyoming* in 1809; from 1820 to 1830 Campbell edited *The New Monthly Magazine.* He died in 1844 and was buried in Westminster Abbey.

For the origin of YE MARINERS OF ENGLAND see note on Martin Parker (1635) and *English Anthology,* pp. 335–7. Campbell had heard an intermediate version sung (to music written by Dr. Calcott) in 1804.

1800. Thomas Moore (1779–1852)

THOMAS MOORE, a musical Irishman of diminutive stature, published his *Odes of Anacreon* in 1800, and *Poems of the late Thomas Little* in 1801. They were a fashionable success, but his *Odes and Epistles* (1809) were cut up in *The Edinburgh Review.* Moore challenged Jeffrey to fight, and thereby gained his friendship and an excellent advertisement. His *Irish Melodies* appeared between 1807 and 1834, and *Lalla Rookh* in 1817; these brought him the then unparalleled sum of £16,000. In 1811 he became Byron's friend, and in 1830 published his *Life and Letters of Lord Byron.*

AT THE MID HOUR OF NIGHT is an experiment in " stressed verse." See the note on Coleridge (1798), his Preface to *Christabel,* and the note on Robert Bridges (*post,* p. 83).

1800. Maria Edgeworth (1767–1849)

MARIA EDGEWORTH, a born story-teller, published her first and best novel, *Castle Rackrent,* in 1800, *Irish Bulls* in 1802,

and *Belinda* in 1803.   They gave her a great reputation in
Ireland, England and France, increased by two series of *Fashionable Tales* (1809–1812).   Scott, whose *Waverley* did not appear
till 1814, declared that he owed his impulse in part to her,
and in 1825 he came to Edgeworthstown to see her.

1802. William Cobbett (1762–1835)

COBBETT, the son of a farm-labourer, and at one time a sergeant
in the British army, began writing in America (*Peter Porcupine's
Journal*).   He returned to England in 1800, and in 1802 made his
mark by producing his *Weekly Register*.   His best work is in
his *Rural Rides* (1830), described in admirable and " sturdy "
English.

1805. Sir Walter Scott (1771–1832)

SCOTT, after collecting the *Minstrelsy of the Scottish Border*
(1802–3), published his own *Lay of the Last Minstrel* in London
in 1805, and its success determined his career.   *Marmion* followed
in 1808.   Scott then completed Strutt's unfinished mediæval
story *Queenhoo Hall* (with an interesting Preface); and published *The Lady of the Lake* in 1810, with unexampled success.
Waverley, the first of his novels, appeared anonymously in 1814,
and he went even further than Swift (see note on *Gulliver*,
ante, 1710, and the letters in *English Anthology*, pp. 452–4), in
denying the authorship of his own work.   (He wrote to Mrs.
Slade, " As I am *not* the Author of *Waverley*, nor in any way
connected with these very successful novels," etc.)   The other
novels were all written between 1816 and 1829.

" When Scott died, his was doubtless the strongest naturalistic influence in Europe.   All the romances of Alexander
Dumas and Victor Hugo sprang directly from him; he had
inspired Fouqué in Germany, Manzoni in Italy, and Fernan
Caballero in Spain " (E. Gosse).

The famous lines, SOUND, SOUND THE CLARION, were long
attributed to Scott, but have lately been discovered to be
a single stanza of a poem by General Mordaunt, used by Scott
as a chapter heading, with the slight change in the second line
of " To all," instead of " Throughout."

1807. Charles Lamb (1775-1834)

CHARLES LAMB, whose farce *Mr. H.* had been hissed in 1806,
made (with his sister Mary) a popular success in 1807 with
Tales from Shakespeare. In 1808 appeared *The Adventures of
Ulysses* and *Specimens of the English Dramatic Poets.* In 1820
The London Magazine invited Lamb to contribute the papers
afterwards republished as *The Essays of Elia* (1823). These were
very favourably received, and *The Last Essays of Elia* were added
in 1833. But even these famous books are for many surpassed
by Lamb's charming letters, the most delightful ever written in
English. It is unfortunate that they have been much garbled
by editors, and the originals are now in America. By the kindness of Mr. N. Haskell Dole the second edition of the *English
Anthology* gives for the first time in this country the true (and
very characteristic) reading of the sentence in the Letter to
Thomas Manning (*English Anthology*, p. 660) on the eleventh
grade of Lamb as a possible " accession of dignity."

1807. George Crabbe (1754-1832)

CRABBE, brought up in poverty first as errand boy and then
as surgeon's apprentice, came to London at 24 and published
a poem, *The Candidate,* anonymously in 1780. It failed, but
he wrote to Burke, who introduced him to Reynolds, Thurlow
and Fox. In 1781 he published *The Library* anonymously, and
in 1783 *The Village,* with his name. These are admirable, but
they did not help him, and he took Holy orders. In 1807 he
made a success with a volume of *Poems* and a long poem, *The
Parish Register.* Finally *The Borough* (1810), *Tales in Verse*

(1812) and *Tales of the Hall* (1819) made him famous and widely popular. His verse descends from that of Dryden, but his themes are modern: his stories are natural, admirably told, and often with great humour.

1810. Charles Wolfe (1791–1823)

WOLFE, a young Irish clergyman who produced only one well-known poem and died at 31, is ignored by some historians of English literature. But *The Burial of Sir John Moore* was immensely popular from the first, and was attributed to Byron, who in disclaiming it told Shelley that he " should have taken it for a rough sketch of Campbell's." For a more just and generous account of it see Professor Elton's *Survey of English Literature,* 1780–1830. Different dates are assigned to the first publication of the poem (Professor Elton 1814, Mr. Gosse 1817, etc.). It is possibly therefore misplaced here.

1810. Robert Southey (1774–1843)

SOUTHEY'S reputation rests upon his *Curse of Kehama* (1810), the finest of an immense series of immense epic poems published between 1801 and 1814. He wrote much for the new *Quarterly Review*; and in 1813 succeeded Pye as Poet Laureate. In the same year appeared his prose masterpiece, *The Life of Nelson.*

THE PILGRIMAGE TO WATERLOO is one of his best minor poems, and has a curious and fresh interest for the present post-war generation.

1811. Jane Austen (1775–1817)

In 1811 JANE AUSTEN made her first appearance in print, with *Sense and Sensibility* (written 1797). This was followed in 1813 by *Pride and Prejudice* (written 1797), *Mansfield Park* (1814), *Emma* (1816); and *Persuasion* (written 1817) and *Northanger Abbey* (written 1798) were published in 1818, after her death. " She is the mother of the nineteenth-century novel, as Scott is the father of it" (Saintsbury).

1814. Leigh Hunt (1784–1859)

LEIGH HUNT, editor of *The Examiner* 1808 to 1821, was imprisoned in Surrey Gaol 1813–15. He made a poetical reputation with *The Feast of the Poets* (1814), *The Descent of Liberty* (1815), *The Story of Rimini* (1816) and *Foliage* (1818). He was taken up by Keats, Lamb, Shelley and Byron, and became the leader of " the Cockney School." From 1828 to 1838 he made successive failures with periodicals, but regained success, as an essayist, with *Imagination and Fancy* (1844), *Men, Women and Books* (1847), *A Jar of Honey from Mount Hybla* (1848) and his *Autobiography* (1850).

1816. Major - General Sir W. F. P. Napier (1785–1860)

NAPIER served through the Peninsular War in the Oxfordshire Light Infantry of the famous Light Division. He began his historical notes in 1816, and his *History of the War in the Peninsula,* when it appeared in successive volumes (1828–40), proved him to possess a genius for military history superior to that of Southey and even of Scott.

1816. Ebenezer Elliot (1781–1849)

ELLIOTT was known for some interesting verse by 1816, and achieved a special reputation by his *Corn-Law Rhymes* in 1828. He owed something to Campbell, and more to Crabbe. His " humane rage " was admired by Carlyle.

1817. John Clare (1793–1864)

Clare, the Northamptonshire Peasant Poet, who lived in the deepest poverty and died after having been many years in an asylum, cannot be said to have ever reached a position of literary influence. His strange poetical career began in 1817 when he printed "Proposals for publishing by subscription a Collection of Original Trifles on Miscellaneous Subjects, Religious and Moral, in verse, by John Clare of Helpstone." The poems were inquired for and at last published in 1820 and well reviewed. Neglect and financial troubles followed the brief success; the poet went back to the land and tried to sell his poems from house to house; illness and insanity followed. It was not until 1908 that a real estimate of his work was published by Mr. Arthur Symons. In 1920 *John Clare : Poems chiefly from MS.* was published (by Mr. Blunden), and the English public recognised the peculiar charm, minutely beautiful vision, and pathetic power of an almost forgotten poet.

1818. George Gordon Byron, Lord Byron (1788–1824)

BYRON's life might be divided into two periods: the first began with his *Hours of Idleness* (1807), derided in *The Edinburgh Review*; *English Bards and Scotch Reviewers* (1809), a piece of successful but crude satire, mostly recanted afterwards; some cantos of *Childe Harold* (1812), a piece of sentimental autobiography, eagerly devoured by the public; and a series of tales in verse, *The Giaour, The Bride of Abydos* and others (1813–16). Then came scandal, unpopularity and exile, during which *Manfred* was written and another canto of *Childe Harold*. At the height of this period of precocious notoriety Byron was in England the rival of Scott, and his reputation at any rate might well be dated from 1812.

But his wider and more lasting fame began later, in the period of his reckless and wilfully romantic Italian wanderings, " the birth-hour of his deeper soul and genius." In 1815 he published *Beppo*, finished *Mazeppa* and began *Don Juan*. In 1819 the Guiccioli adventure followed. In 1820 he wrote *Marino Faliero, The Prophecy of Dante* and the fourth and fifth cantos of *Don Juan*. In 1821 his *Cain* and in 1823 his fine satire, *The Vision of Judgment*, outraged and exasperated public feeling in England. But it was during these five years of amazing vigour and growth that his genius established on the Continent an empire only paralleled by that of Shakespeare himself. Professor Elton, in his detailed study of Byron (*Survey of English Literature*, 1780–

1830, pp. 135–182), attributes this to the combined effect of his Titanic rebelliousness, his satiric but powerful observation of life in *Don Juan*, and his fame as the liberator of Greece and champion of insurgent nationalities. Such fame as this is out of sight of the precocious audacities of the young nobleman of 1809 and 1812.

1818. John Keats (1795–1821)

KEATS was adopted by Leigh Hunt and " the Cockney School " in 1816; his first *Poems* failed in 1817. In 1818 he burst into full flower with unparalleled suddenness, published *Endymion* and wrote *The Eve of St. Agnes* and *Hyperion*. In 1819 he wrote the *Ode to a Nightingale*, the *Ode on a Grecian Urn*, the *Ode to Autumn*, *Isabella*, *Lamia*, the *Eve of Saint Mark* fragment and the revised portion of *Hyperion*; these were published in July 1820. In February 1821 he died in Rome.

Keats assimilated many influences: the outline of the Greek art, the romantic colour of the Ballads, Ariosto and the Elizabethans, the metrical style of Chaucer, Dryden and Gray. His own influence on English poets is unequalled—he is one of the " full-welling fountain-heads of change."

1819. Percy Bysshe Shelley (1792–1822)

SHELLEY came suddenly to public notice in 1819, when he was violently attacked in *The Quarterly Review*. He had already published, without any effect or attention, *Queen Mab* (1813), *Alastor* (1816) and *Laon and Cythna* (1817). *The Cenci* (1819) and *Prometheus Unbound* (1820) were followed by *Adonais* (1821). Many other poems, including the six wonderful lyrics here given, were only published after his death. He inherited and bequeathed far less of his qualities than many lesser poets: naturally, for he is essentially " fire and air " and these are not transmissible.

1821. Walter Savage Landor (1775–1864)

LANDOR is not easy to place, for he had an ineffective early poetical period of nearly a quarter of a century. He had made a name in one way and another by 1821, when he settled in Florence and entered upon his vast enterprise, the *Imaginary Conversations*. These appeared between 1824 and 1829, and brought him the recognition of the critics. *The Pentameron* was published in 1837. His prose is still read, but his lasting fame rests upon his small gem-like poems, which have in the highest degree the classical and Jonsonian elegance.

1822. Thomas Love Peacock (1785–1866)

PEACOCK wrote imitative verse for some years and then spent fifteen years in perfecting a new type of satirical novelette. The series, *Headlong Hall* (1816), *Melincourt* (1817) and *Nightmare Abbey* (1818), was crowned by *Crotchet Castle* in 1831, and this last year, in the best opinion of to-day, is the date of Peacock's arrival at maturity. But his contemporaries took less pleasure than we do in these exquisite classics, and were more attracted by *Maid Marian* (1822) a " comic romance " or rather comic operetta in prose and verse, which has a double interest —it links *The Beggar's Opera* with *The Pirates of Penzance,* and it gives a most entertaining transposition of *Ivanhoe,* which appeared in December 1819, and (in spite of Peacock's mistaken recollection) evidently suggested a great part of it.

1822. Thomas Lovell Beddoes (1803–49)

Dream-Pedlary   738

BEDDOES published *The Bride's Tragedy* in 1822; his *Death's Jest-Book* and *Poems* were both published after his death by suicide in 1849. The Jacobean dramatists, Cowley and Shelley, were his masters.

1822. Winthrop Mackworth Praed (1802–39)

The Vicar   738

PRAED, " a schoolboy and undergraduate of genius," had made a reputation by 1822, and in the following year published his *Lilian.* His popular and inimitably witty light verse was only collected in 1844, five years after his premature death. He is the ancestor of Barham, and also of the more modern school of J. K. Stephen, Quiller-Couch, Owen Seaman and Alfred Cochrane, the last of whom resembles him in outlook as well as in versification.

1822. William Hazlitt (1788–1830)

Nether Stowey and Linton (*Winterslow*)   .   .   741

HAZLITT was diverted from the ministry to letters by the visit to Coleridge and Wordsworth recorded in the extract given here. He produced articles and lectured on the poets till he was well over 40. He then wrote at Winterslow the two famous volumes of *Table Talk* published 1821–2. The *Liber Amoris* (1823) and *The Spirit of the Age* (1825) were followed by a complete failure with a *Life of Napoleon Buonaparte* (1828–30) and by his death in the latter year.

1825. Thomas Babington Macaulay (1800–59)

MACAULAY made his reputation at the age of 25 with his first article in *The Edinburgh Review*, 1825 (on Milton). In 1830 he entered Parliament, and after a brilliant career in England and India, published his famous *Critical and Historical Essays* in 1841 (in America), his equally famous *Lays of Ancient Rome* in 1842, and his *History of England* in 1848.

1827. George Darley (1795–1846)

DARLEY, between some early verses and later dramas, published two remarkable volumes in *Sylvia* (1827), a fairy play, and *Nepenthe* (1839), an unfinished rhapsody: both are full of passages of rare and original beauty. The lyric here given is memorable not only for its own sake, but as having suggested to George Meredith both the music and the theme of his *Love in the Valley*.

1827. Thomas Hood (1798–1845)

HOOD made his living as a professional jester, but his best work is both thoughtful and deeply pathetic. His chief publication is his *Plea of the Midsummer Fairies* (1827), dedicated to his friend Charles Lamb: but he also wrote a number of beautiful and famous songs.

1827. Thomas De Quincey (1785–1859)

By 1827 DE QUINCEY had distinguished himself in the three lines most characteristic of him: he had published (at first anonymously) his imaginative *Confessions of an English Opium-Eater* (1821), his *Dialogues of Three Templars* (1824) on political economy, and the first of his imitations and translations of

E

German romance. Later came his *Autobiographic Sketches* and a set of articles on his friends Wordsworth, Coleridge and Lamb. The *Confessions* he greatly enlarged and republished in 1856.

1829. Francis Jeffrey (1773–1850)

PAGE

Felicia Hemans (*Edinburgh Review*, Oct. 1829) . 754

JEFFREY cannot be said to have any separate literary existence in the ordinary sense, but he put forth from 1802 to 1829 a kind of " official criticism " and may be considered to have established his claim to remembrance before he gave himself up to the law, which made a judge and a peer of him. He furnishes this Anthology with a review and sample of Mrs. Hemans' once famous work, not otherwise exemplified here.

1829. Captain Frederick Marryat (1792–1848)

The Genteel Boatswain (*Peter Simple*) . . 757

MARRYAT's first and one of his most famous stories was *Frank Mildmay* (1829). Perhaps *Peter Simple* (1834) is his masterpiece—or *Mr. Midshipman Easy* (1836); but he enjoyed a deserved and still unexhausted popularity from the first, and has never had a rival.

1832. Benjamin Disraeli, Earl of Beaconsfield (1804–81)

Tadpole and Taper (*Coningsby*) . . . 760

DISRAELI made a sensation in 1826 with *Vivian Grey*, but his real reputation began with *Contarini Fleming* in 1832. Of the others, those which have worn best are *Venetia* and *Henrietta Temple* (1837), *Coningsby* (1844), *Sybil* (1845) and *Lothair* (1870), and they enjoy to-day an even more serious admiration than when their insight had yet to be approved by the course of history.

1832. Edward Bulwer Lytton, Lord Lytton (1803–73) ·

The Final Shock (*The Last Days of Pompeii*) . 763

LYTTON is chiefly remembered for his novels *Eugene Aram* (1832), *The Last Days of Pompeii* (1834), *The Last of the Barons*

(1843), *The Caxtons* (1849), *My Novel* (1853) and *Kenelm Chillingly* (1853); and his play *The Lady of Lyons* (1838). He passed from Byronics to historic " tushery," and so to the domestic and autobiographical: his last style was his best, but the earliest the most popular.

1833. Henry Wadsworth Longfellow (1807–82)

LONGFELLOW gave up poetry very early—he had been imitating " his favourite poets from Gray to Byron "—and at 24 had begun writing essays in *The North American Review* (1831). By 1833 he had made a name, and was publishing travel sketches in *The New England Magazine*—reprinted in 1835 as *Outre-Mer: a Pilgrimage beyond the Sea*. He turned again to verse in 1837, and with *The Reaper and the Flowers* and *The Psalm of Life* at once convinced the public on both sides of the Atlantic. He lived to write far better poems than these, and became immensely popular. Opinion is now less favourable to him; but *My Lost Youth*, here given, is an irresistible example of his charm.

1833. Thomas Carlyle (1795–1881)

CARLYLE wrote for the *Edinburgh* from 1827, and in 1833 his *Sartor Resartus* began to appear serially in *Fraser's Magazine*: the first step in his lifelong mission of bringing the German mind to the understanding of the English. The *French Revolution* (1837), the *Life and Letters of Oliver Cromwell* (1845) and the *Life of Friedrich II.* (1858–65), proved him the first historical genius of his time.

1853. Charles Kingsley (1819–75)

KINGSLEY'S fame will always rest on his two brilliant novels, *Hypatia* (1853) and *Westward Ho!* (1854). By a regrettable mistake of one figure he has been placed in the *English Anthology* at the date 1833.

1833. Ralph Waldo Emerson (1803–82)

EMERSON resigned the pastorate of the Second Church, Boston, in 1832: he had been writing poetry for some years, and his famous *Good-bye, Proud World* was in 1833 generally believed to refer to this change in his career. A denial has been published: but in any case the existence of the legend proves his repute at this time. In 1835 he settled at Concord, which thereupon became " The Delphi of New England," and on the next anniversary of the Concord fight he published the celebrated verses on " the embattled farmers " who " fired the shot heard round the world." He was afterwards known all over the English-speaking world as a philosopher and essayist, and was an intimate friend of Longfellow, Carlyle, Lowell and Thoreau.

1833. Alfred Tennyson, Lord Tennyson (1809–1892)

TENNYSON was only 24 when his fame was established by his second volume of *Poems* (1833). It contained, among many wonderful pieces glowing with a kind of Pre-Raphaelite beauty, the second and third here given, *The Lady of Shalott* and the choric song of *The Lotos-Eaters*; our first, *Mariana*, had been published in 1830. The fourth, an echo of Webster, appeared in *The Germ*. In his boyhood Tennyson worshipped Byron: but he was soon seen to be far nearer to Keats. Afterwards he ransacked the classics (*e.g. Lucretius* and *Tithonus*), Dante (for *Ulysses*) and the great English lyrists (see note on Sidney, and Carew's " Ask me no more," *English Anthology*, p. 338, etc.).

1839. Edgar Allan Poe (1809–49)

In 1839 POE published in Boston his *Tales of the Grotesque and the Arabesque,* followed by *The Gold Bug* and an article on Cryptography. In 1841 he published a prediction of the plot of *Barnaby Rudge,* deduced from the introductory chapters, which is said to have caused Dickens to ask Poe if he was the devil. *The Murders in the Rue Morgue* appeared the same year. In 1845 he made his poetic fame with *The Raven,* immediately reprinted in a volume with the same name; but *Annabel Lee* afterwards surpassed it in popularity. Poe's view of poetry was a perverse one; he declared that beauty was its sole object, and also that " a long poem is a contradiction in terms." He himself aimed " not to tell a story but to produce an effect: and in poetry not to convey an idea, but to make an impression." The influence of this theory may be clearly traced in R. L. Stevenson's work.

1837. Charles Dickens (1812–70)

DICKENS took his place among the great creators when he published *The Posthumous Papers of the Pickwick Club,* in 1837. He was for the remaining years of his life by far the most popular writer of the age, and his books are powerful to-day as far as Russia and the cities of China.

1839. Charles Darwin (1809–82)

DARWIN'S first publication was *A Naturalist's Voyage Round the World* (1839), better known as the *Voyage of the " Beagle."* This is from the literary point of view as good as anything he ever wrote; the passage here given is a vivid description of the islands where the *Emden* met her fate on November 9, 1914. An idea which had occurred to Darwin during his voyage in the *Beagle* was afterwards followed out in *The Origin of Species* (1859), a book of world-wide and lasting fame.

1843. Walt Whitman (1819–92)

In 1843 WHITMAN, who had been a printer, schoolmaster, editor, carpenter and builder, published a wonderful poem in a wholly new mood and manner, with the title of *Blood-Money.* Here, in lines of the now famous unprosodical cadence, is the democratic or humane passion expressed already with perfect simplicity and success. Remembering this, I have made the mistake of assigning Whitman's first influence to the same year as that of Ruskin and of Mill. He would be more consistently placed in 1855, when his *Leaves of Grass* brought him fame and vituperation at once, and gave him potent influence— for both good and ill—in the development of English poetry. (Professor Santayana writes of *The Poetry of Barbarism* [*Whitman and Browning*] in *Poetry and Religion,* 1900.)

1843. George Borrow (1803–81)

BORROW made his reputation in 1843 with his *Bible in Spain,* an original and entertaining book of travel. His more imaginative works, *Lavengro* (1851) and *The Romany Rye* (1857), are both picturesque and valuable for their scenes of gipsy life.

1843. John Ruskin (1819–1900)

RUSKIN'S *Modern Painters* (1843) was published without his name, but speedily gained for him a reputation greater than that ever enjoyed by any other writer on art in this country. Vols. III. and IV. were added in 1856 and Vol. V. in 1860.

1843. John Stuart Mill (1806–73)

MILL lives by his *System of Logic, Ratiocinative and Inductive* (1843), his *Principles of Polical Economy* (1848) and his *Liberty* (1859): works not only scientifically important but written with admirable clearness and vigour.

1844. Elizabeth Barrett Browning (1806–61)

ELIZABETH BARRETT's two volumes of *Poems*, published in 1844, " placed her for the first time among the foremost living poets " (E. Gosse). " There is scarcely any writer in English deserving the name of poet, who illustrates by defect the importance of poetic style so well as Mrs. Browning " (G. Saintsbury). But her *Sonnets from the Portuguese*, written to Robert Browning during their engagement (1846) have never suffered detraction, and the earlier part of *Aurora Leigh* (1856) remains delightful reading.

1847. Charlotte Brontë (1816–55)

The vivid, obscure, pathetic lives of the three Brontë sisters make up one of the great stories of the literary world. In 1846, as " Currer, Ellis and Acton Bell," they failed with a joint volume of *Poems*. In 1847, in circumstances of great distress, Charlotte (Currer) published *Jane Eyre*, Emily (Ellis) *Wuthering Heights*, and Anne (Acton) *Agnes Grey* (which she followed up in 1848 with *The Tenant of Wildfell Hall*). In December 1848 Emily died, and Anne in May 1849; Charlotte in complete loneliness wrote *Shirley*. *Jane Eyre* had been completely successful from the first. She now went to London and Brussels, published *Villette* in 1853, married in 1854, and died in 1855. Her books are filled with an intensity of feeling and pictorial power unknown till then in English fiction.

1847. Emily Brontë (1818–48)

EMILY BRONTË was a less competent novelist than Charlotte, but an even more powerful one. There is no forgetting " that sinister and incongruous but infinitely fascinating tragedy," *Wuthering Heights*. Greater still and more certain of perpetual fame are her poems: the two here given are among those which for perfection of form, expressing profound spiritual emotion, must always be counted among the greatest we possess.

1848. William Makepeace Thackeray (1811–63)

THACKERAY wrote from 1836 in *Fraser's Magazine* and *Punch*, but it was not till 1847–8 that he suddenly achieved an immense success with *Vanity Fair*. *Pendennis* followed in 1849–50, and *Esmond*, his second masterpiece, in 1852. *The Newcomes* (1853–55) and *The Virginians* (1858–9), the *Cornhill* essays called *The Roundabout Papers* (1860–2) and the burlesque fairy-tale *The Rose and the Ring* (1855), all contributed to give Thackeray a reputation in England and America which challenged that of Dickens.

1849. Arthur Hugh Clough (1819–61)

CLOUGH is a more interesting poet than some who have been more completely successful in expression. His most popular poem is his original and entertaining *Bothie of Tober-na-Vuolich* (1849). It is criticised for the "badness" of its hexameters: but Clough showed in his still more charming verse-novel *Amours de Voyage* that he thoroughly understood Latin prosody and used it as he chose. The first of the short poems here given has long been in all anthologies: the second makes an interesting comparison with the "Whither, O Splendid Ship" of Mr. Bridges.

Clough died in 1861, and his friend Matthew Arnold honoured him with his beautiful *Thyrsis*—the elegy which by common consent makes a third with *Lycidas* and *Adonais*.

1854. Cardinal John Henry Newman (1801–90)

NEWMAN'S reputation during his life was rather that of a theologian and controversialist than a literary man: yet both his prose and verse always had distinction. His name as a writer will be remembered for his volume on *The Idea of a Catholic*

University (he was appointed rector of the new Roman Catholic University in Dublin, in 1854), his *Apologia pro Vita Sua* (1864) and his hymn " Lead, kindly light."

1854. Frederick Tennyson (1807–98)

FREDERICK TENNYSON was Alfred's eldest brother: the first of his poems were included in the *Poems by Two Brothers* (1826): the best were published in his own volume *Days and Hours* (1854).

1854. Coventry Patmore (1823–96)

PATMORE made his name in 1854 with *The Angel in the House,* a domestic story in verse, raised and beautified by interludes of lyric epigram. These original and unsurpassed pieces delighted Ruskin, Bridges and other friends and critics; but the whole poem has been decried by many and mercilessly parodied by Swinburne. *The Unknown Eros* (1877) and other poems are more difficult but not less distinguished.

1855. Robert Browning (1812–89)

BROWNING was late in arriving at anything like fame or influence. His first play, *Strafford* (1836), ran for five nights: his long poem, *Sordello* (1840), was received with howls. *A Blot in the 'Scutcheon* (1843) produced only a quarrel with Macready, and in 1852 he was duped into publishing a critical Introduction to a volume of forged " Letters by Shelley." But in 1855, when he and his wife, Elizabeth Barrett Browning, had been living for eight years in narrow circumstances in Italy, his

Men and Women finally carried conviction and cast a favourable light back upon the *Dramatic Lyrics* of 1842 and *Dramatic Romances* of 1845—evidences which, as Mr. Saintsbury says, " should have settled the question " before. *The Ring and the Book* (1868), in four volumes and 20,000 lines, is a dramatic story of crime and helpless innocence, treated with an inexhaustible humanity and a profound psychological insight which have never been equalled in poetry.

Browning was for many years pitted against Tennyson, as Dickens was against Thackeray, by their contemporaries and partisans. The perfection of Tennyson's form (which is no superficial matter) will save his best but not probably the larger part of his work. Browning's strength does not lie there (though his form *is* the true expression of his spirit), but in his extraordinary intensity and sincerity of feeling and thought. Where Tennyson looks on and judges life from a refined and at times even sentimental retirement, Browning goes down into the fight or the carnival, " sublimating passion and creating truth."

1855. Anthony Trollope (1815–82)

Who shall be Cock of the Walk? (BarchesterPAGE

Towers) 856

ANTHONY TROLLOPE began the series of his admirable and successful novels with *The Warden* (1855) and *Barchester Towers* (1857). *Framley Parsonage* was commissioned by Thackeray for the new *Cornhill* (1860), and *The Last Chronicle of Barset* appeared in 1867: perhaps the best of all.

1855. Matthew Arnold (1822–88)

The Scholar-Gipsy.   860
The Function of Criticism (*Essays in Criticism*) . 867

! MATTHEW ARNOLD'S *Strayed Reveller* attracted little attention in 1849, and his *Empedocles on Etna* (1852) was speedily withdrawn from circulation. His position as a poet was secured in 1855, when he completed the issue of his two volumes of *Poems*. In 1857 he became Professor of Poetry at Oxford; and in 1865 appeared his famous *Essays in Criticism*. His best verse has a charm of an unusual kind: a mixed descent may be traced from the Greek tragedies, from Spenser, and from Heine.

1858. William (Johnson) Cory (1823–92)

WILLIAM CORY (born Johnson) published in 1858 the first part of his *Ionica*—short poems full of classical beauty and romantic ardour.

1859 (1850). Nathaniel Hawthorne (1804-64)

HAWTHORNE's greatest book, *Transformation* (originally drafted as *The Marble Faun*), was finished in 1859 and published in Boston and London in 1860. But he was already famous as the author of *The Scarlet Letter*, a gloomy study of New England Puritanism (1850), and of *The House of the Seven Gables* (1851), and *The Blithedale Romance* (1852). For the great influence of his original and imaginative quality see the note on Shorthouse, *post*, 1880.

1859. George Meredith (1828–1909)

GEORGE MEREDITH made his fame as a novelist with *Richard Feverel* (1859) and as a poet with *Modern Love* (1862), a story of tragic misunderstanding told in a sonnet-sequence of extraordinary power. His novels owed something to the work of his father-in-law Peacock (*supra*, 1822, and *English Anthology*, pp. 730–7). His own prose style has influenced many writers, (see Mr. Maurice Hewlett's *The Stooping Lady*): his poetry towards the end of the century succeeded Browning's as the gospel of the rising generation.

1859. Edward FitzGerald (1809–83)

FITZGERALD's *Rubáiyát of Omar Khayyám* was published in 1859. Though unsuccessful until rediscovered by Rossetti,

Houghton and Swinburne, and not popular until years afterwards, it is the everlasting monument of his fame: a work of original genius, built out of fragments from the Persian, and bringing an entirely new influence into English poetry.

1861. Charles Reade (1818–84)

PAGE

Several of CHARLES READE'S books achieved wide popularity, his *It is Never too Late to Mend* as early as 1856. But *The Cloister and the Hearth* (1861) is one of the greatest historical novels ever written and gives him his place in literature.

1861. Christina Rossetti (1830–94)

CHRISTINA ROSSETTI, sister of D. G. Rossetti, contributed (as "Ellen Allegra") to the Pre-Raphaelite *Germ* in 1850; but reached her high position by her *Goblin Market and Other Poems* (1861), which contained all four of the exquisite pieces here given. Her greatness lies not in her superiority to all her predecessors of her own sex, but in the new beauty and depth of emotion which she joined to the mystical piety of the school of Vaughan and Crashaw.

1860–5. Thomas Henry Huxley (1825–95)

HUXLEY'S greatest and most lasting influence dates from the years 1860–5, in which he not only championed the cause of Darwin as no one else could have done, but published a remarkable series of essays and addresses fearlessly applying the principles of Cartesian criticism and contending for freedom of thought in that direction. The directness, lucidity and unconscious elegance of his style may be judged from the extract here given: no Englishman has ever written or spoken so well on scientific subjects.

1865. Algernon Charles Swinburne (1837–1909)

SWINBURNE first intoxicated readers of poetry in 1865 with his *Atalanta in Calydon*, the like of whose choruses had never been heard in English verse. In 1866 his *Poems and Ballads*, like a beaker full of the warm South, produced an even stronger effect. This volume contained *The Triumph of Time*, from which nine famous stanzas are here taken. *Tristram of Lyonesse* (1882) should be compared with Matthew Arnold's *Tristram and Iseult* (1852), Tennyson's *Last Tournament* (1872); and Mr. Laurence Binyon's *Death of Tristram* in his *Odes* (1901).

1866. William Morris (1834–99)

WILLIAM MORRIS published in 1858 *The Defence of Guenevere*, the firstfruits of a new and splendid genius which had not yet ripened. In 1866 he reaped a full harvest with *The Life and Death of Jason*: in 1868–70 he showed himself to be the direct (and the greatest) descendant of Chaucer, by producing the four volumes of *The Earthly Paradise*, a vast series of classical and romantic tales, the like of which are not to be found in English. In 1873 appeared the fascinating mystery-play *Love is Enough*:

in 1877 *Sigurd the Volsung,* the most heroic and faultless of the few epics we possess. In 1891 he collected in *Poems by the Way* the shorter pieces of his last poetical period, and showed a new and even deeper originality.

His seven prose romances—*The House of the Wolfings,* etc. (1889–98)—are almost equally distinguished: they too combine his romantic charm with his peculiar intensity of imagination. Their English is a fifteenth-century style adapted to scenes mainly of a Scandinavian character. Another mood produced the wonderful mediæval *Dream of John Ball* (1888) and the prophetic dream of *News from Nowhere* (1891), embodying the Socialistic faith of a heart too noble for the world of his time: the only great allegorical pieces since *The Pilgrim's Progress.* The marvellous fantasy of colour and sound called *The Hollow Land* he contributed to *The Oxford and Cambridge Magazine* in his undergraduate days, and it was only reprinted after his death.

See notes on Lord Berners, *ante,* 1523, and More, 1535.

1858. " George Eliot " (1819–80)

PAGE

Miss Brooke and Mr. Casaubon (*Middlemarch*) .   923

" George Eliot " (Mary Ann Evans) fulfilled the promise of her *Scenes of Clerical Life* (1857) by the complete success of her *Amos Barton* (1858), *The Mill on the Floss* (1860) and *Silas Marner* (1861). She reached the summit of popularity by the publication of *Middlemarch* (1871), a novel of unsurpassed power in the delineation of provincial English society and the characters moving in it. She is here placed too late, as Kingsley is placed too early, by a typographical error of a single figure. It is greatly regretted that (after 900 pages) the proof-corrector should have nodded: and equally that of many thousand readers, not one (in twelve months) should have observed and pointed out the mistake.

1869. James Anthony Froude (1818–94)

An Estimate of Disraeli (*Life of Benjamin Disraeli*)   931

Froude from 1867 was writing his admirable *Short Studies on Great Subjects,* but they were not collected till 1883. Meanwhile he made his reputation by his *History of England from the Fall of Wolsey to the Defeat of the Armada* in twelve volumes, completed in 1869. A more popular success was his *English Seamen in the Sixteenth Century.* A brilliant, inaccurate, pugnacious writer, with a great natural gift of style.

1870. Dante Gabriel Rossetti (1828–82)

ROSSETTI (Gabriel Charles Dante, known as Dante Gabriel) wrote some of his best poems before 1862, but in that year buried the MS. in his wife's grave. Seven years afterwards it was disinterred by permission of the Home Secretary, and the *Poems* were published in 1870. Rossetti, who had been a cofounder of the Pre-Raphaelite Brotherhood in 1849, was already a famous painter, and was now recognised as a poet of genius. *The Blessèd Damozel* is his most admired single poem; *The Portrait* his best and most profoundly sincere; but his fame lives in his *House of Life,* a sonnet-sequence which stands nearest to Shakespeare's own.

1872. Andrew Lang (1844–1912)

ANDREW LANG was a many-sided and gifted man of letters who made his mark as a writer of delicate verse in old French forms. His *Ballads and Lyrics of Old France* (1872), *Ballades in Blue China* (1880), *Rhymes à la Mode* and *Ballads and Verses Vain* (1884) all had an immense vogue, and with his literary essays, studies in Scottish history, the Greek Epic and political biography, gave him the character of an Admirable Crichton. The first sonnet here given was first printed at the beginning of the masterly *Translation of the Odyssey* (1878), in which he collaborated with Professor Henry Butcher.

1872. Thomas Hardy (born 1841)

MR. HARDY's fame as a novelist began with his *Under the Greenwood Tree* (1872) and *A Pair of Blue Eyes* (1872–3); the great series of seventeen volumes ended with *Jude the Obscure* (1895) and *The Well-Beloved* (1897, a reprint). As a poet he only became known in 1898, when his *Wessex Poems* (written 1865–97) appeared; they were followed by *Poems of the Past and Present* (1901). Then came the gigantic " epic-drama " *The Dynasts* (1903, 1906, 1908); then *Time's Laughing-Stocks* (1909), *Satires of Circumstance* (1911 and 1914) and *Moments of Vision* (1917). *The Dynasts* stands alone in English literature and no extract of moderate length could do it justice; but by Mr. Hardy's generosity and personal help we have here one of his most characteristic prose scenes and a set of fifteen shorter poems which well illustrate one side, and many different lights and shades, of his genius. He ranges in these from the sombre Æschylean mood, in which he has many times appealed for Man against his gods, to a rare joy of life and an exquisite tenderness of love. Throughout his work he is like Shakespeare in more ways than one: he is essentially moral in his judgments of life; yet he makes his sun to shine upon just and unjust alike : he is like him also in two special gifts—in his absolute possession of the landscape and the humour of the English

countryside, and in the power of making lyric beauty out of
common words. His best poems are of that highest order,
whose magic lies in " the sound of the meaning "; his best
prose is a part of the deeper history of his own country.

1873. Austin Dobson (1840–1921)

DOBSON, like Lang, was first known as a writer of finely
wrought verse: *Vignettes in Rhyme* (1873), *Proverbs in Porcelain*
(1877), *Old-World Idylls* (1883), *At the Sign of the Lyre* (1885)
—the well-chosen titles characterise the contents, but cannot
convey the extreme charm and delicacy of the talent they
exhibit—the talent of a fine workman " whose limitations were
never known because he never exceeded them." His Essays
have the same exquisiteness of urbanity and scholarship.

1873. Edmund Gosse (born 1849)

MR. GOSSE was Dobson's junior by nine years, but his contemporary in literature and at the Board of Trade. He too
first came forward as a poet: his five volumes, *On Viol and
Flute* (1870), *King Erik* (1876), *New Poems* (1879), *Firdausi
in Exile* (1885), *In Russet and Silver* (1894), were collected into
one in 1896, and admirably exemplify his wide culture and
fastidious workmanship. His prose work includes Lives of
Gray, Cowper, Donne, Jeremy Taylor, Sir Thomas Browne
and Swinburne, and many volumes of literary essays, some of
which—*e.g., Critical Kit-cats* (1896), *French Profiles* (1905),
Portraits and Studies (1912)—are brilliant examples of a new
biographical method, personal, picturesque, and highly finished.
In his unique *Father and Son* (1907), which was crowned by
the French Academy in 1913, he carried this method to the
extreme of perfection, painting both his subject and himself
at once.

1873. Walter Horatio Pater (1839–94)

PATER's inspiration came from Ruskin, but his *Studies in
the History of the Renaissance* (1873) revealed a very different

F

style and philosophy, and became at once a *causa belli* among critics and moralists. Equally original, fascinating and perturbing were his *Marius the Epicurean* (1885), *Imaginary Portraits* (1887), *Appreciations* (1889), *Plato and Platonism* (1893) and *Greek Studies* (1895). The verdict of the public was that he was a Decadent who gave new life to English culture, and a Euphuist whose characteristic style was of a grave and religious beauty.

1875. Henry James (1843–1915)

HENRY JAMES gained a reputation and a certain measure of popularity with his novel *Roderick Hudson* (1875), afterwards concluded in his *Princess Casamassima* (1886). These and others of their period are brilliant and lucid stories of character, but James's subtle curiosity and multiple insight demanded a more complete expression of shades and values which few but himself perceived. His later books were more and more relished by the few and derided by the many. *The Sacred Fount* (1901), *The Wings of the Dove* and *The Golden Bowl* (1905) form perhaps the shibboleth of this battle; but like other shibboleths it may be disregarded (as such) by all who choose to be non-combatants. Henry James did much for the novel of character; and in spite of his objective and almost surgical method, he has left in his work the record of a great and charitable nature as well as of a highly original artistic impulse.

1878. Robert Louis Stevenson (1850–94)

STEVENSON (Robert Lewis Balfour, afterwards called Robert Louis) wrote in magazines for some time before he published *An Inland Voyage* (1878) and *Travels with a Donkey* (1879). Essays followed, then the *New Arabian Nights* (1882) and *Treasure Island* (1883). These all formed a *crescendo* of success, and R. L. S. was the most popular writer of his time when he produced in rapid and profitable succession *Prince Otto* (1885) (originally drafted as *Semiramis : a Tragedy*), *Dr. Jekyll and*

Mr. Hyde (1886), *Kidnapped* (1887), *The Black Arrow* (1888), *The Master of Ballantrae* (1889) and *Catriona* (1893). In 1887 *Memories and Portraits* appeared, and a volume of verse, *Underwoods*, both full of personal charm. In 1889 Stevenson went to live in Samoa, where he wrote two memorable volumes, *A Footnote to History* (1892) and *Island Nights' Entertainments* (1893), and the delightful *Vailima Letters*, published in 1895 after his death.

Stevenson pleases most when he is most himself, least when he is too visibly concocting effects of style. He has told us in the Essay on *A College Magazine* of his early habit of "playing the sedulous ape" to the masters of the past. He was only doing what Ben Jonson advised (see the passage on style in *English Anthology*, p. 255), but the result in many places—and even in his fine fragment *Weir of Hermiston* (1893-4)—is a sudden suspicion of something histrionic or affected, a jar to the affectionate admiration of his most attached readers. If only he had lived to write "A Footnote to the History of Style"!

1880. William Ernest Henley (1849–1903)

HENLEY made his name between 1877 and 1890 as a journalist and editor of uncommon style and vigour. His Poems (1888, 1898, 1901) are spirited and at times exquisite. His rather overdone masculinity was due no doubt to his own physical disability and suffering, endured with exasperated fortitude.

1880. Robert Bridges (born 1844)

Most of MR. BRIDGES' great qualities appear in his sonnet-sequence *The Growth of Love* (1876)—his antique grace, his modern subtlety, and the grave beauty of his thought, enhanced by its union with a masculine joy and faith. But he was almost unknown until after the publication of his famous *Shorter Poems* in three Books (1873, 1879, 1880), to which a fourth was added in 1890 and a fifth in 1893. These were not only of wide range and full of curious felicities, but the originality of both their subjects and rhythms brought a new freedom into English poetry. Mr. Bridges, who is the most learned and acute prosodist we have yet had, and an accomplished student of music, has a sense of rhythm and a love of metrical experiment which have at times taken him a little in advance of the more old-fashioned of his audience: but he has received the fitting recognition of his genius in his appointment to the Poet Laureateship and in the unanimous acclaim of his younger contemporaries in the Commonwealth of Poetry.

1880. Joseph Henry Shorthouse (1834–1901)

SHORTHOUSE gave to the world in 1880 the book which (by no desire of his own) had been laid by for many years in a privately printed edition. When at last it appeared, *John Inglesant* brought to its author perhaps the most unhoped-for tribute of praise ever won by a work of fiction in modern England. The book is called by Shorthouse himself " a Philosophical Romance," and he adds that the threads of it are " the conflict between Culture and Fanaticism—the analysis and character of Sin—the subjective influence of the Christian Mythos (Eternal Truth manifested in Phenomena)." To the reader it is a powerful vindication of the position of the historic Church of England, cast into the form of a dramatic story, the two acts of which are laid, one in the England of the Civil War, the other in the Italy of the post-Renaissance period. The writer owns an obligation to Hawthorne's " art carried to perfection," but he has fully equalled his model in the mature and melancholy beauty of his style, and has even surpassed him, to the mind of most Englishmen, in the interest of his thesis and the profound sincerity of his eloquence.

1897. Mary Coleridge (1861–1907)

MARY COLERIDGE, great-niece of S. T. Coleridge, made her reputation in 1897 by her first historical romance *The King with Two Faces*. Her poems appeared in small volumes without her name, in 1896–7–8, and in periodicals from 1900 to 1907: a collection from these and from her MSS. was published (in 1907) after her death. Her work was immediately successful both with the general public and with the best living imaginative writers. Their critical studies of her poems noted her affinity with Coleridge, Blake, Heine and Christina Rossetti, but her not less striking originality, her wide range and intimate sincerity. "They will be her portrait, an absolutely truthful picture of a wondrously beautiful and gifted spirit, whom thought could not make melancholy nor sorrow sad; not in conventional attitude, nor with fixed features, nor lightly to be interpreted, nor even always to be understood, but mystical rather and enigmatical; a poetic effigy, the only likeness of worth" (Robert Bridges).

INDEX